The Food We Eat, the Stories We Tell

New Approaches to Appalachian Studies

Series editors: Elizabeth S. D. Engelhardt, Erica Abrams Locklear, and Barbara Ellen Smith

Gone Dollywood: Dolly Parton's Mountain Dream, by Graham Hoppe

The Food We Eat, the Stories We Tell: Contemporary Appalachian Tables, edited by Elizabeth S. D. Engelhardt with Lora E. Smith

The Food We Eat, the Stories We Tell

Contemporary Appalachian Tables

Edited by Elizabeth S. D. Engelhardt
with Lora E. Smith

With an Afterword by Ronni Lundy

OHIO UNIVERSITY PRESS • ATHENS

Ohio University Press, Athens, Ohio 45701
ohioswallow.com
© 2019 by Ohio University Press

To obtain permission to quote, reprint, or otherwise reproduce
or distribute material from Ohio University Press publications, please
contact our rights and permissions department at (740) 593-1154 or
(740) 593-4536 (fax).

Printed in the United States of America
Ohio University Press books are printed on acid-free paper ⊗ ™

29 28 27 26 25 24 23 22 21 20 19   5 4 3 2 1

Library of Congress Cataloging-in-Publication Data
Names: Engelhardt, Elizabeth S. D. (Elizabeth Sanders Delwiche), 1969-
  editor. | Smith, Lora E., 1979- editor.
Title: The food we eat, the stories we tell : contemporary Appalachian
  tables / Edited by Elizabeth S. D. Engelhardt with Lora E. Smith ; With
  an Afterword by Ronni Lundy.
Description: Athens : Ohio University Press, [2019] | Series: New
  approaches to Appalachian studies | Includes bibliographical references.
Identifiers: LCCN 2019028620 | ISBN 9780821423912 (hardcover) | ISBN
  9780821423929 (trade paperback) | ISBN 9780821446874 (pdf)
Subjects: LCSH: Food habits--Appalachian Region, Southern. |
  Cooking--Appalachian Region, Southern. | Appalachian Region,
  Southern--Social life and customs.
Classification: LCC GT2853.U5 F67 2019 | DDC 394.1/20975--dc23
LC record available at https://lccn.loc.gov/2019028620

This book is dedicated to the next generation

of Appalachian foodways scholars, writers,

cooks, artisans, farmers, seedsavers, and

advocates—*journey strong.*

Contents

Contents

Acknowledgments

This book would not be possible without the care and skillful attention of Gillian Berchowitz at Ohio University Press. Thank you for believing in our vision and shepherding this collection to print. Thank you to the authors included in this collection for sharing your intellect, research, wit, and stories. Our field is richer for your voices. A deep bow of gratitude to the foundational work to document and advance the study of Appalachian foodways by Ronni Lundy and Fred Sauceman. We stand on your shoulders and hope this collection invites more scholarship and inquiry into mountain foodways. And a special thank-you to the members of the Appalachian Food Summit for your ongoing work to create community and conversation through the stories of regional foodways.

Introduction

Two Walnuts, a Piece of Quartz, a Pencil, Dad's Pocketknife, and a Quarter: Things I Carry

Elizabeth S. D. Engelhardt

THE WRITER Ursula K. Le Guin did not live in Appalachia. I don't know if she ever visited Mount Mitchell in North Carolina or Mount Le Conte in Tennessee. I don't know if she ever rested at the Peaks of Otter in Virginia or passed through the high country of West Virginia. I do know she lived in Portland, Oregon, within the large footprint of Mount Saint Helens, the volcano she called her neighbor in the Cascade mountain range of Washington. When Mount Saint Helens erupted in 1980, Le Guin was at the forefront of writers connecting ecology to literature to resilience and nature's power in mountain communities. She passed away in January 2018, so we cannot ask her about the relation between eastern and western mountains and the cultures living with them. But we can say Le Guin defined herself with her mountains.

Le Guin also knew storytelling. In 1986, Le Guin wrote an essay entitled "The Carrier Bag Theory of Fiction."[1] I've been thinking about her piece during quiet moments this winter and spring. It's an essay meditating on the shapes of the stories we tell. She invites us to picture the arc of the flight of an arrow, with all its straightness, hardness, rise, fall, and penetration. That hunting arrow describes a dominant western popular culture definition of what a great story needs: vigorous action, a sharpened point, and the ability to wound, penetrate, or even kill. Its flight—rising high into the air, climaxing, falling back to earth—traces classic advice for action, climax, denouement from countless writing manuals and high school English class textbooks.

That's not the storytelling Le Guin finds compelling. She calls instead for stories that take the shape of the humble carrier bag. A bag is useful and practical; things in a bag brush up against each other and are always in relation to each other and to the container itself. Bags, with the things we carry in them, give us context and histories and possibility for futures. Novels, she argues, work best as containers. The novels she likes have beginnings without defined endings; the characters don't see everything clearly always; and they have space to avoid "linear, progressive, Time's-(killing)-arrow."[2] They have people wandering around, bumping against each other, doing deeply human things in them. To Le Guin, this is the power of a novel and of storytelling; this is the version that can reveal us to ourselves.

I'm not sure I've ever seen Le Guin discussed in the circles of food studies to which I belong and with which the authors included in this volume are in conversation.[3] But "The Carrier Bag Theory of Fiction" lists in its opening paragraph "the vegetable," as well as "seeds, roots, sprouts, shoots, leaves, nuts, berries, fruits, and grains" as the items which kept early humans alive—and the things put into actual carrier bags over time. She notes that we might be tempted to overemphasize the protein on a plate, whether from hunting or fishing, because its path to the meal might have been a more action-packed dynamic one, involving those arrows both literal and metaphorical. But, she argues, the foods that actually sustain and maintain humans on a daily basis are the ones gathered, collected, held in the carrier bags of communities. The final lines of the essay, after Le Guin has mapped her own vision of a more expansive, realistic, and deeply human version of fiction, remind us that "still the story isn't over. Still there are seeds to be gathered, and room in the bag of stars."[4]

APPALACHIAN food and the people who grow, cook, preserve, sell, reject, transform, eat, and write about it exist in relation to mountains. Those mountains are physical—they shape the ecologies of weather, water, soil, and life. Mountains are also cultural and metaphorical, constructed by social communities talking about them. What can be grown, what can be raised, what can be preserved and how, all is determined in some relation to mountains and hills. What tastes good, what is emblematic, what is avoided, and who gets a voice in deciding, all too develop with mountains in the discussion. Even in our stories of how people in Appalachia or connected to Appalachia try to avoid those mountains—whether by building transportation systems to ship foods from elsewhere, by reshaping the earth itself, by leaving or being pushed out, or by leveraging our identities in other racial, ethnic, or national cultures that bridge highlands and lowlands—those people are doing so because of the stubbornly powerful presence of the mountains themselves.

Mountains are here, in the pieces that follow. Many of the authors or their families come from mountain communities of North Carolina, Kentucky, West Virginia, Tennessee, Virginia, and the ongoing Cherokee and other indigenous groups' lands created before and lasting after those state lines were drawn—or they find themselves working in or with communities of people who once lived in Appalachia. Some of the authors trace family and personal global migrations to and from towns and cities in Spain, South Korea, Mexico, and Switzerland. Detroit, Alabama, and New York, among other US origins and destinations, make appearances. New home communities that are queer, multiracial, and marked by shared creative practice bring mountains to life in memory and daily life even for contributors who live in places that feel unconnected from their Appalachia. Of course, your personal most important mountain or idea of mountains may not be in this list of places. Perhaps you are reading this in South Carolina or western Maryland. Perhaps you belong to a Kentucky social club in Los Angeles. Perhaps your mountains contain stories of Brazil or a religious community or a newspaper's voice. It is the accumulation of mountains that matters, not the comprehensive definitions.

EFFORTS to make single definitions—to outline the Appalachian region or the Appalachian story—historically have looked much more like the hunter's odyssey that Le Guin decried. Stories about Appalachia, if they take the shape of that arrow's flight, become stereotyped tragedies of the region's fall or of an individual's quest to rise or escape. Yet there is a different version of telling stories in Appalachia, one that allows many mountains, many objects to be carried around.

Even so, we ought to stay clear-eyed and brutally honest about the objects in Appalachian carrier bags. A pocketknife might cut an apple to share—but it equally can be a weapon to wound or kill. Appalachian rocks, minerals, water, and land have been stolen, reclaimed, and stolen again. Technologies, including humble pencils, have the power to shape and erase people, places, and knowledge, even as they can be tools for creation and unsilencing. Guessing wrong can kill us and the ones we love. Few human actions have higher stakes than the decision to trust, to find partnership; trust and alliance require continual renewal as we brush up against each other, objects, and ideas.

For some of us, weighing the safe and the dangerous might be what is said between the words shared in a story well told. Ronni

Lundy describes the wooden table around which her family sat when she was a child. The stories told there narrated what her father saw on a given day. They had a shape, but that shape was not a straight line. They had a teller, but he invited others—cousins, visitors, Ronni herself—to participate as well. Ronni's description has also been on my mind this spring, as I just returned from a family funeral. I found myself replying to friends who wanted to know how I was doing by saying, "We are a porch-sitting people." I meant: The funeral service was short and kind but also awkward for us as a group to fit what we needed into its form. The memories and the reshaping and reforming of our extended family took place in the hours after the service, when we sat on my cousin's screened-in porch, nestled into the side of a mountain, and just told stories. Stories without beginnings and without ends; stories that included the person now gone and stories that she would have enjoyed hearing. Both Ronni's and my experiences sound a lot like Le Guin's novel-as-carrier bag. The stories about and in Appalachia that begin with the carrier bag are the stories to tell, the stories that make communities and futures.

The pieces here start at different moments in time. Erica Abrams Locklear and Lora E. Smith write about the 1940s and 1950s. Michael Croley, Robert Gipe, and Emily Wallace write about the 1970s and 1980s. Jessie Blackburn and William Schumann, Courtney Balestier, Annette Saunooke Clapsaddle, and Daniel S. Margolies begin their stories after 2000. Pieces from Rebecca Gayle Howell and Emily Hilliard stand outside a strict chronology and instead look to memory and moment. They certainly do not end in the same place—or at all. The gardens and their produce that feature in entries by Karida L. Brown, Abigail Huggins, and Danille Elise Christensen are still evolving and being discussed. Crystal Wilkinson, Suronda Gonzalez, and Jeff Mann dwell in the in-between spaces of possibility. Many mountains, then, are joined here by many stories.

LE GUIN'S loving description of a plate of vegetables and foods from seeds saved and ingredients gathered could just as easily come from the menu of one of Appalachia's most thoughtful restaurants today. Heritage beans and other vegetables, apples and other fruits and nuts, all carefully grown and preserved from seeds, saplings, roots, and cuttings by people who know the differences between and among hybrids, figure strongly in the Appalachian foodways of these pages. Difficult conversations about foraging and gathering in public forests or of endangered and picky plants stand behind the quieter emphasis here on gardens or grocery stores. Seasonal ingredients, which downplay a star entrée and elevate the multitude of sides, play important roles in the vivid descriptions of actual tables and daily eating. But Le Guin's words also work as a metaphorical description of the mixtures of old and new, local and global, practical and fanciful, cheap and expensive, fraught and accepted, hardly noticed and intentional that mark how actual communities in the United States navigate the foods we eat—with all the intersecting layers of identity, power, injustice, and privilege that make up life today, including lives in Appalachia.

The definition of Appalachian foodways across these stories and mountains may surprise. It includes Taco Bell, very expensive wines from French varietals, and frozen foods from the national grocery chain down the road. It features yellow eye and shucky beans carefully saved by loving gardeners, but it also values pinto beans from the local Costco in Michigan. It celebrates 150-year-old recipes but welcomes cooks who have scribbled Crisco substitutions in the margins. It invites us to really see what is on a table—and in a car and in a care package shipped from afar. It invites us to keep exploring the Appalachianness of foods, the stories of mountains, and the global foods of Appalachian eaters.

THIS book is a carrier bag. Each essay is an object knocking around within it. The objects include a *Searchlight Cookbook* produced in the Midwest but used in Kentucky; a door frame to a mother's house; the cardboard box designed to survive the modern grocery store's frozen food section without destroying the fried chicken it held; the salt shaker carried in a back pocket because the whole community's tomatoes are coming in; the tortillas folding around the region's tacos; the dish on the table for a family's chowchow; the packets holding seeds ready to be planted in one's own and others' gardens; the long-handled spoon perched at ready on the buffet line; the cup and dipper for a cold sip of water; the Cool Whip container holding precious leftovers five hundred miles from home; the fast-food architecture of Taco Bell; hot dog signs and buildings; a pickled Band-Aid; a glass jar; a pan carried from Spain; the label on a bottle of Appalachian wine; a rosette iron; a feather and blade.

This may be an unsettling introduction. I am not giving you the sight line along which to aim your arrow or tracing the arc it will follow. I am not putting myself in the works that unfold so you can walk the same path. We have not self-divided the pieces into discrete thematic sections that artificially separate some pieces from others. In her afterword, Ronni does not describe her journey through the pages for you to retrace in her wake. Instead, I invite you to brush up against the essays, the creative pieces, their authors, and their objects. I encourage you to wander around in here, reading forward, around, backward, or repeatedly. I ask you to look in your own bag to see what you are carrying today. I invite you to take out the stories and objects here one at a time or by the handful. I invite you to tuck them away into your own carrier bag and take them into your own story. Appalachian food, Appalachian stories, Appalachian objects—mountain food, stories, and objects that are also national and global food, stories, and objects—might just brush up against each other in ways that help us imagine futures in which it is possible to survive and thrive with resilience, in a robustly diverse ecology of nature, people, with a couple of recycled plastic containers, and even a few stars.

NOTES

1. Ursula K. Le Guin, "The Carrier Bag Theory of Fiction," in *Ecocriticism Reader: Landmarks in Literary Ecology*, ed. Cheryll Glotfelty and Harold Fromm (Athens: University of Georgia Press, 1996), 149–54.

Elizabeth S. D. Engelhardt

2. Le Guin, "The Carrier Bag Theory of Fiction," 153.

3. Le Guin's work helped shape ecocriticism, an academic movement that took hold in the 1980s and 1990s; she has been a strong voice in certain US feminist conversations. Those two communities—ecocritics and feminists—are kin to food studies in the humanities, certainly. See, for instance, Allison Carruth, *Global Appetites: American Power and the Literature of Food* (Cambridge: Cambridge University Press, 2013) and Alison Hope Alkon and Julian Agyeman, eds., *Cultivating Food Justice: Race, Class, and Sustainability* (Cambridge, MA: MIT Press, 2011).

4. Le Guin, "The Carrier Bag Theory of Fiction," 149, 154.

Chapter 1

The Household Searchlight Recipe Book

Lora E. Smith

I COME from a place of dumpling makers. I live in an economy built on fried squirrel, frog legs, fruit cobblers, and the shared work of women's wisdom and hands. A region shaped by a piecrust made of 3 cups flour, 1 cup lard, 2 teaspoons of salt, and ½ cup or so of water. I know these things because they are scribbled down in the margins of my great-grandmother's cookbook.

I was gifted a 1938 copy of *The Household Searchlight Recipe Book* by my mother after my second child, a son, was born. I'd just moved home to eastern Kentucky for what I'd sworn was going to be the very last time. The cookbook originally belonged to my great-grandmother and namesake, Lora Sharp, and had been handed down to my grandmother and then to my mother. It now rests inside a Ziploc bag I keep on the top shelf of my pantry.[1]

The Household Searchlight Recipe Book was part of a series of cookbooks targeted at women living in towns of ten thousand people or less released during the 1920s through the 1940s. The cookbooks were published by the Topeka, Kansas–based *Household Magazine,* a monthly women's magazine that promised to address the needs of its (largely white and rural) readership. "The Household Searchlight" was a regular column in the magazine that tested and rated new consumer products for the home.

The February 1926 issue of the magazine has the author of that column testing a new Nesco stove with the opening proposition that "a stove needs to perform so many duties in a kitchen that the selection of a new one is indeed a problem." The same issue also contains a full-page advertisement for Jell-O that excitingly proclaims, "So easy to prepare that even the children can make it." And an editorial titled "Women at Home—and Out of It" discusses technological advances alongside promoting policy change to increase immigrant labor as an "economical" means for relieving the demands of domestic work on white women starting to enter jobs in a changing economy.[2] Domesticity, home economics, and to a larger extent the changing role of rural white women in an industrializing workforce had become modern problems in need of modern solutions. In this case, solutions included the exploitation of immigrant labor, processed foods potentially prepared by children, and technology in the form of expensive consumer goods like new washing machines and vacuums.

The *Household Searchlight Recipe Book* in my possession was developed by open-sourcing recipes from its national readership through a reported one thousand questionnaires that were mailed to identified subscribers, "who were known to be especially interested in food preparation." The resulting book was divided into a "General Directions" section organized by technique and a "Recipes" section organized under twenty-two different tabs categorized by type of food. The cookbook's foreword lets the reader know that expert help is close at hand:

> The Household Searchlight is a service station conducted for the readers of The Household Magazine. In this

seven-room house lives a family of specialists whose entire time is spent in working out the problems of homemaking common to every woman who finds herself responsible for the management of a home and the care of children.[3]

The recipes come from women such as Mrs. J. F. Deatrick of Defiance, Ohio, who shares her self-proclaimed "Prize Winning Recipe" for Turnip Cups.

Select white turnips of equal size. Pare. Cut a thin slice from the top of each, so turnips will stand when inverted. Parboil in salted water. Drain. Beginning at the bottom, hollow out each one in the form of a cup. Mash the portions of turnips which were removed. Combine with an equal quantity of chopped meat, cheese, or fish. Season to taste. Moisten with a little cream. Place in a baking pan. Bake in moderate oven (375 F) about 25 minutes. Serve with roast or boiled mutton or beef.

Mrs. R. J. McLin of tiny Hazel Green, Kentucky, shares a Pineapple Fluff recipe that includes egg whites, whipping cream, crushed macaroons, jelly, crushed pineapple, diced marshmallows, and grated sweet chocolate.

Combine egg whites and jelly. Beat until stiff. Fold in stiffly whipped cream, pineapple, and macaroons. Add marshmallows. Pile lightly in glasses. Dust with chocolate. Serve ice cold. If desired, lady fingers or vanilla wafers may be substituted for macaroons.

Virginia Cooper of New Orleans, Louisiana, an urban anomaly in the collection, is especially prolific, making an appearance in almost every section to share dishes like Creole Gumbo and Creole String Beans. There are other regional dishes sprinkled throughout the book, including recipes for tomato gravy, hominy, hassenpfeffer, and chili con carne.

But the copy pressed into my hands by my mother was not a standard edition. Brown tattered edges of papers stuck out in every direction, and the spine of the book was almost threadbare. Upon opening up its black embossed cover that shows a small home nestled beneath trees, I discovered that my great-grandmother had been using the cookbook as a personal diary in which dates, mundane happenings, and important events were recorded alongside family and community recipes.

Sometimes the included recipes are transposed on top of the cookbook's "official" printed recipes, my great-grandmother's handwriting completely covering the front and back covers of the book as well as taking up white spaces of pages therein. Scrawled in the margins like graffiti and taped to the backs of pages like wheat-pasted city flyers, her family's and neighbors' recipes take up room throughout the cookbook and often stand in contrast to the printed recipes that signal a middle-class and pre-Depression abundance. A recipe written in blue ink on a piece of yellow paper taped over an Index page shares a Depression-era pie that approximates crackers for cooked apples.

Ritz Cracker Apple Pie.

> Bring to a boil.
> 2 cups water. Add
> 1 ½ " sugar.
> 1 stick butter
> 2 ½ teaspoons cream tarter.
> ½ " nutmeg.
> After this mixture has come to a boil, drop in
> 26 to 30 whole Ritz Crackers.
> Cook 2 minutes.
> Then pour in unbaked pie
> shell that has been sprinkled
> with cinnamon, bake 450
> for 20 or 30 minutes, or until
> brown.

Some of these recipes are noted as Lora's, but most are attributed to other women—family members, friends, and neighbors. Dot's Chili, Mrs. Logan's Prune Cake, and Mrs. Jack Skinner's Icicle Pickles share equal top billing. There is variety but also duplication in many of the recipes. There are multiple pickle recipes, layer cake recipes, and hot roll recipes. Some are almost identical, but all are attributed to different women in her community and show respect by being chosen as important and "good enough" to be saved.[4]

And then there are the journal entries. Dates, places, names, events. My great-grandmother utilized the commercially produced cookbook as a private space to chronicle her life, making visible a network of friends, family members, neighbors, and daily occurrences, tucked in somewhat haphazardly among the chattering recipes from strangers. The journaling allows me to create a sense of chronological order to her days and may have served as a way for her to make sense of her life—one marked by loss from an early age.[5]

Lora Skinner was fifteen years old in 1903 when she died during childbirth on her family's farm in Whitely County, Kentucky. Her parents, Alice Hatfield and Greenberry Skinner, were raising four children on a subsistence farm located up a holler near Rockholds, Kentucky, when Lora became pregnant out of wedlock. The father was unknown, or at least his identity was kept from the rest of the family and treated as a shameful secret. Even in my generation we were told not to discuss it. On the recorded birth certificate, the father of the child is listed as John Sharp, a fifty-four-year-old neighbor who lived in the holler over from the Skinner farm. It's possible that he was the father. Or maybe the father was John's twenty-year-old son. What tugs at me is whether this was a pregnancy resulting from an act of young love or from the rape of a teenage farm girl left to fend for herself amid long days of labor.

Upon birth, my great-grandmother Lora Sharp was given her dead mother's first name and the surname of the man who reluctantly claimed her, and was raised alongside her aunts and uncles on the family farm. Her mother is not buried in the hilltop family graveyard in Woodbine, Kentucky, where Alice, Greenberry, and their other three children rest. In fact, after searching historical records and physically searching the family cemetery and surrounding cemeteries in the community, I have been unable to locate any grave at all. Lora Skinner disappeared from the family after giving birth to her daughter, and I've accepted that her name is likely as close as I'll ever come to her.

Seven-year-old Lora Sharp was enumerated incorrectly in the 1910 Census under her mother's name, Lora Skinner, and was also mistakenly listed as a niece rather than a granddaughter. The 1910 Census also lists several nonfamily members as "boarders" living in the house with Lora and her family. One boarder in the home is Bradley Brooks, a seventeen-year-old African American boy born in Kentucky. Bradley is gone from the Skinner home by the 1920 Census, and I have yet to locate him again in historical records.[6]

At nineteen, Lora Sharp moved off the farm to the railroad town of Corbin, Kentucky. There she married her first husband, an engineer on the L&N Railroad with whom she had her only child, my grandfather Ora Moss Smith. Lora divorced several years later and, according to her cookbook diary in an entry that reads unceremoniously, "Bob and I was married May 4, 1936," became Mrs. Bob Meadors. At the same time, Lora took in Bob's son Dillard to raise. Everyone on my side of the family agreed that Bob was from Ohio, a polite way of saying that no one liked him. The two remained married until Lora's death in 1975.

The original diary entries that are visible in the cookbook mostly revolve around my grandfather Ora Moss Smith's time deployed during World War II. Lora writes as an anxious mother of an only child documenting letters, wired messages, and bits of news they received from or about my grandfather. My grandfather, thankfully, came home, intact and honorably discharged with a Purple Heart, but suffering with malaria and signs of PTSD from his deployment in the Philippines. An entry written vertically in looping cursive near the spine of the front cover reads, "Ora come back from San Diego, Calif. December 15, 1942 Discharged."

However, an entire page of dates and journaling has been covered by two pieces of butcher paper glued on top. One of the brown pieces of paper has an orange cake recipe and the other a recipe for fermenting pickles with wild grape leaves added as a tannin-containing agent, a mountain trick to keep pickles crisp in the crock. Maybe she didn't care to lose some things to a good pickle recipe. But judging from the few dates and scribbles that are visible beneath the butcher paper, I believe Lora was writing multiple entries about time periods she purposely wanted to cover up because they chronicle her first marriage. I worked with an archivist at University of North Carolina at Chapel Hill's Wilson Library to try and remove those pieces of butcher paper, but with no luck. Lora chose to paste over that part of her life, and I am forced to respect that she didn't want me to see what she didn't want me to see.

But something else is happening on the inside cover that puzzles me. Lora documents her birthday every year usually with some piece of quantitative data attached to it: where she lived, what she weighed, the destination of a trip, or a visit by a family member or friend that occurred. It's odd, but I believe what she was ultimately doing was marking time. And it's not lost on me that her birthday each year also commemorated her mother's passing, a passing she had no way of outwardly memorializing because there was no graveside to visit and the circumstances of her birth and her mother's death were muffled in the family's silence.

Through her marked and altered cookbook, Lora actively defined a regional identity and economy grounded in Appalachian foodways through her choices of go-to recipes. Immediately noticeable upon encountering the cookbook are the dog-eared pages and brightly inked circles and stars surrounding printed recipes in the cookbook she liked and, I assume, used often. They include many of the meals I grew up with as a young child during family suppers in the 1980s. Likewise, almost all of the circled recipes are familiar southern or Mountain South ones, or they are adaptable enough to her home, based on readily available ingredients. In the Game section, Fried Squirrel and Squirrel Stew are circled with vigor, both recipes hailing from women in Appalachian Ohio. Squash dishes are starred and highlighted over and over. Several familiar quick breads in the Breads section stand out, and Frog Legs is the only thing circled in the misidentified Fish section.

Recipes she added that are especially stressed are Lora's "dumplins" recipe and her pie crust recipe. Dumplins are so important that a reminder of what page number they are on—it's page 256—graces both the front and back inside covers. The recipe is written in fuchsia ink as follows:

(Dumplins)

2 cups flour
Stir make hole
2 table spoons lard
½ teaspoon salt
1 teaspoon Baking ~~Powder~~ Powder
2 eggs in tea cup.
Finish up with water & make your dough.
That is Dumplins

What you're supposed to do afterward to complete the recipe is not clear, so the women in my family learned directly from one another or improvised and innovated to our own taste.

Taken together, the many voices of the women held inside the worn leather cover—Lora's voice, the voices of women in her local community, and the national network of readers of *Household Magazine*—create an effect that says, "We are here. We existed. Remember us." It's an affirmation of lives lived in and outside rural kitchens. It's an accounting of women's daily uncompensated invisible labor and value. And it's hidden in plain sight on a kitchen counter within the pages of a cookbook.

In "'Beyond the Mountains': The Paradox of Women's Place in Appalachian History," Appalachian studies scholar Barbara Ellen Smith uses family narratives and material culture to challenge

16

what she terms Appalachia's "fraternity of the frontier." Smith argues that male-dominated frames of agency have largely been responsible for the creation of the images and history of Appalachia. Smith writes that, in order to counter such histories and frames, scholars must take an "approach that looks beyond orthodox sources of data and fields of action to locate women's history-making and the contestations of gender."[7]

Smith's colleague and collaborator, scholar Patricia D. Beaver, expands on the idea: "As Appalachian history has been constructed out of masculinist narratives, Smith argues that inclusion of female agency in that history challenges our 'most common and cherished assumptions' about the region that are part of the 'mesmerizing loci of patriarchy as historical truth.'" Beaver concludes, "Broadening the concept of agency to include women's critique and challenge of power, particularly through hidden transcripts of subversion, illuminates the anti-isolationist emphases that are revealed in women's networks of domestic production and exchange."[8] Lora's *Searchlight* cookbook is one of the unorthodox sources of data and hidden transcripts that Smith and Beaver ask scholars and writers to consider.

It is a place where my great-grandmother engaged daily with history making through recipe and diary. It speaks directly to the anti-isolationist experience of an early twentieth-century Appalachian economy and regional identity built on networks of rural women's domestic exchange through traded recipes, knowledge, and the sheer fact that store-bought ingredients included commodities like canned oysters and pineapples. Hers was a table serving locally shot Kentucky Fried Rabbit next to crushed Hawaiian Pineapple Sherbet.

It is a site of history and placemaking, where the personal mastery of mountain home cooks challenged the scientific and measured expertise of seven people supposedly living in a lab house. It offers a space where women shared information and my great-grandmother could choose to hide her experiences in plain sight.

It also offers a narrative that prioritizes an economy built on female friendships and family, social networks, collaboration, and cooperation. The national rural and more localized community networks of women sharing knowledge, working collaboratively, and affirming their existence, skill, and labor represented in the pages of my *Household Searchlight Recipe Book* offer a different understanding of eastern Kentucky and a potential model to inform the future of labor and creative placemaking and placekeeping happening now in parts of central Appalachia.

In contemporary eastern Kentucky, local food and agriculture, including culinary arts and foodways, are emerging as one of the most promising sectors in an economic transition rapidly under way following the collapse of the region's coal industry. Leaders like Chef Kristin Smith of the Wrigley Taproom in Corbin, Kentucky; community organizer Valerie Horn of the C.A.N.E. Community Kitchen and Letcher County/City of Whitesburg Farmers' Market in Whitesburg, Kentucky; and social enterprise developer Candace Mullins of Grow Appalachia in Berea, Kentucky, are all weaving new networks. They are utilizing the region's foodways as an economic opportunity for local entrepreneurship while crafting a postcoal cultural identity that centers experience and identity within seed, ingredient, recipe, and women's labor. This new economy I am experiencing and engaging with tastes like a generations-old Turkey Craw bean organically grown by farmer Maggie Bowling and "Mom's Special Curry" noodle bowl at Mae Suramek's Noodle Nirvana restaurant.

From my vantage point working in community economic development, the future of eastern Kentucky is female. It is emerging from local community-based solutions and led by the informal and formal labor of women. Most importantly, these next-generation entrepreneurs are not hiding.

When we center the stories of women and historically marginalized people—including the ones told by contributors to this volume—when we seek out previously hidden or obstructed narratives, new visions and new futures can emerge based on understanding a more accurate and expansive accounting of the past. In moments of political and economic change, stories that challenge older forms of power—power that is decaying—are especially necessary. Stories about Appalachia, like the one present in my great-grandmother's cookbook, provide us with new possibilities for creating the future traditions and knowledge our communities will need to survive.

I come from a place of dumpling makers. I live in an economy built on fried squirrel, frog legs, fruit cobblers, and the shared work of women's wisdom and hands. A region shaped by a piecrust made of 3 cups flour, 1 cup lard, 2 teaspoons of salt, and ½ cup or so of water. I know these things because she wrote them down. I know these things because I remember her.

NOTES

1. This creative nonfiction essay is taken from ongoing research for a thesis project that examines the role of recipe and ingredient in forming notions of Appalachian regionalism and cultural identity. The full work pulls from interdisciplinary scholarship in American studies, Appalachian studies, feminist studies, and folklore. For purposes of this essay, I am positioning the southern recipe as rhetoric that functions as a "role builder" of cultural identity and place. See Ashli Quesinberry Stokes and Wendy Atkins-Sayre, *Consuming Identity: The Role of Food in Redefining the South* (Oxford: University Press of Mississippi, 2016).

2. *Household Magazine* 26, no. 7 (February 1926), http://memory.loc.gov:8081/gc/amrlgs/hm1/hm1.html.

3. "Foreword," *The Household Searchlight Recipe Book* (Topeka: Household Magazine, 1936), n.p.

4. While not strictly fitting the description of a "community cookbook," Lora's text does include similarities, namely the repetition of recipes attributed to different friends and family members in her community. See Anne L. Bower, ed., *Recipes for Reading: Community Cookbooks, Stories, Histories* (Amherst: University of Massachusetts Press, 1997).

5. For a discussion of cookbooks used as scrapbooks and texts by women to give structure and order to their daily lives, see Janet Theophano, *Eat My Words: Reading Women's Lives through the Cookbooks They Wrote* (New York: Palgrave, 2002).

6. Bradley Brooks's presence in the home challenges the narrative of eastern Kentucky as exclusively white. Future research of his residency and role in the house is planned for what it could reveal about black life and race relations in rural southeastern Kentucky during the period. His exit by the 1920 Census is of particular interest to me as Corbin, Kentucky, the county seat of Whitley County and the nearest incorporated town to the Skinner farm, was the site of a 1919 race riot that earned Corbin the reputation for being a flash point for racism and racial violence in southeastern Kentucky. See "Kentucky Town Re-examines Its Racial History," National Public Radio, March 10, 2007, https://www.npr.org/templates/story/story.php?storyId=7772527.

7. Barbara Ellen Smith, "'Beyond the Mountains': The Paradox of Women's Place in Appalachian History," in "Appalachia and the South: Place, Gender, Pedagogy," special issue, *NWSA Journal* 11, no. 3 (Autumn 1999): 1–4.

8. Patricia D. Beaver, "Women in Appalachia and the South: Gender, Race, Region, and Agency," in "Appalachia and the South: Place, Gender, Pedagogy," special issue, *NWSA Journal* 11, no. 3 (Autumn 1999): xix.

Poem

Clearing Your House

(for my mother)

George Ella Lyon

> "I kissed all the doorways."
> 　　　　—Jan Cook

the strongbox that holds fifty unidentified keys
and the certificates for our polio vaccinations

the box of blank key tags

the carved wooden chest, shoebox size, brim
with shoelaces, window shade brackets,
a Chappell's Dairy pencil, a wooden shoe
a bicentennial key ring

castanets, rattlesnake rattles
and an irradiated dime from Oak Ridge

the linen closet where, among blankets and sheets,
I find the sheet music to "Abilene"

the kitchen cabinet where my grandmother's
mixing bowls bought from the Jewel Tea man
hold two fistfuls of rolled coins and the rest
of the medicine that saved you in 2006

the drawer where I find teacups among the linens

a leather binder with all the records
from the March of Dimes in 1959

the towel cabinet
which falls out of the wall
when I clear out the towels
the Christmas tree sheet-shrouded
wedged against the pipes behind it

the desk drawer jammed with chess pieces
straight pins, loose slides, and the map folder
—Detroit, Toronto, New York—from vacation, 1954

the avalanche of photos from shoeboxes,
envelopes, drawers: sepia, deckle-edged tintype
none labeled
            those three little girls
            wearing their daddy's hats
            fading out of a faded world
            are they Ella and Mickey
            and you?

the library sorted into fifty-plus boxes
your Churchill books in one that says
Fruit Loops

Clearing Your House

ledgers, deposit slips

newspaper clippings in desks, in file drawers,
under the directory on the telephone table,
of you, speaking at a meeting,
receiving an award, launching the Christmas parade

the hatchet in the kitchen tool drawer
all those CDs of the Irish Tenors

the grease-and-flour-spotted *Searchlight Cookbook*
the glass canister of pinto beans
the roaster you always mixed
the dressing in

the wall of plaques hung not by you
but by the cleaning lady
who was proud of you

four copper-colored jello molds
two shepherd figurines
the chair Jo "went to housekeeping with"
the nesting dolls which won't unnest
that you brought back from Russia
receipts for that trip
suitcase
guidebooks
passport

your glasses
your checkbook

the last shoes you wore
into the world.

Chapter 2

Setting Tobacco, Banquet-Style

Erica Abrams Locklear

WITH A tinge of criticism in her voice my mother always told me that I "grew up on a sidewalk." As loath as I am to admit it, she was mostly right.

Even though I was raised in a rural area and am a seventh-generation Western North Carolinian, I did not grow up farming. I grew up in a comfortable brick rancher with a carefully manicured lawn and nary a field or garden in sight, though there was a cow pasture across the road. My father—who grew up farming and could build a fence, run a chainsaw, and cultivate a field of greasy cut-short beans with the best of them—rose before dawn every morning to report to his plant-supervisor job forty-five minutes away in Arden. My mother worked part-time at a bank in West

Asheville and kept a meticulously clean home; she often told me about the drudgery of working in the fields that prompted her and her sister to threaten to "set up a tent on Pack Square" in downtown Asheville. My mother couldn't get far enough away from a life dependent on the earth. Conversely, my father was far more nostalgic, regaling me with stories of riding in a wagon with his maternal grandfather, a man born in 1876 who never learned to drive.

But whether remembered negatively or positively, my parents' farming history was not my reality. Even as a child, I lamented that fact. I went to school with children whose families raised tobacco or ran a dairy or both: those kids *knew* things. They could milk a cow. They knew how to hoe potatoes without cutting into them. They had arrowhead collections. They participated in mysterious 4-H activities involving large farm animals. I always had the sense that I was missing out on something important and worthwhile.

So I looked for every opportunity to align myself with that earthy world, hoping to prove to my mother, but more to myself, that sidewalk or not, I could hold my own in the world from which my parents came. I wanted to experience it, to know it: so I ate. One of the best things associated with what seemed like "real" mountain culture was the food. Although the culinary landscape of my childhood was one typical of the 1980s, with frozen dinners, Hamburger Helper, and Little Debbie cakes, I also routinely had access to foods that are now considered—and lauded—as distinctly southern or Appalachian. There was my neighbor's black walnut cake slathered in stovetop caramel icing, Mabel Duckett's ham biscuits so salty they made your mouth pucker, and even the smelly ramps my father loved to eat in the spring. We had giant pots of green beans seasoned with ham hock, thin cakes of cornbread baked in a cast-iron skillet until dark brown, and the occasional pot of creasy greens that left the house smelling for days. But we ate most of these foods seasonally; they did not constitute the majority of our diet. So as I grew up hearing about the plentiful meals both sides of my family had enjoyed after hours spent in the fields, those heaping plates of vegetables, fresh fried chicken, and elaborate cakes took on mythic proportions in my adolescent mind; I even fantasized about cornbread crumbled up in buttermilk and served in a Mason jar for supper. I used to wish we had a spring house instead of a refrigerator.

What's clear to me now is that I was on a culinary search for "authenticity," that elusive term that, according to historian Fitzhugh Brundage, defies definition altogether. Certainly Brundage has a point that "any definition [of authenticity] is likely to provoke the response, 'Authentic compared to what?'"[1] Even so, the concept persists. Food can serve as an essential marker of regional identity, but trying to parse which foods are authentically "mountain" and what the broad term "Appalachian" means are loaded issues. Certainly I identify as Appalachian, but I am also aware that spending the vast majority of my adult life in academia has much to do with that identification. Plenty of people who live in the region often reference their state or county when explaining where they are from. My maternal grandmother, for example, always said that she grew up in Madison County, North Carolina. I do not recall ever hearing her use the term "Appalachian." Even so, most contemporary, mainstream depictions of her would call her Appalachian. That designation, whether or not she would claim it for herself, carries tremendous cultural baggage that lumps together white farmers in Western North Carolina with African American coal miners in West Virginia with Cherokee people in northern Georgia and so many more. Yet despite the diversity of the region, a fairly narrow selection of foods has come to represent it. Some qualify and some do not.

In fact, I suspect that some might scoff at the inspiration for this essay: Banquet frozen fried chicken. Perhaps ironically, in my quest to stockpile mountain credibility, I did so fueled by lunches featuring Banquet frozen chicken as the main dish. Every spring when my maternal grandmother needed help setting tobacco plants, I jumped at the chance to participate. It was perfect: my shoes got dirty, afterward I had to use an old toothbrush to scrub the dirt from under my fingernails, and I was able to sit with my mother on the back of a tractor for hours. We talked, we joked, and

I had a chance to prove that I would not perish after a few hours in the field. Best of all, around 11:00 a.m.—because nobody can work on an empty stomach—my grandmother would stand on the porch and yell that dinner was ready. Dinner, of course, meant lunch, and I loved it.

In her prime, my grandmother would have likely killed a chicken, cleaned it, and fried it; made biscuits from scratch; and served various vegetables that she had put up the previous summer. But by the time I was helping set tobacco, she was crooked over with osteoporosis and not physically able to make such meals, let alone set tobacco. Even so, she took enormous pride in the food that she served and managed to offer many of the same foods she would have once prepared herself, though now I wonder how frequently she offered some of these items. Instead of homemade biscuits, we had canned biscuits, burned to a crispy char on the bottom because the oven door never closed just right. Instead of homemade jelly, we had Garner's, straight from Ingles grocery store. And instead of fresh fried chicken, we had Banquet "fried" chicken. Launched in 1970 by a company founded in 1953, Banquet frozen fried chicken was a staple in my grandmother's kitchen. Baked to crispy perfection on an aluminum-foil-covered pan, it was salty and warm and tasted like crunchy heaven. At the time I never thought much about the fact that she wasn't killing or frying the chicken herself: instead, I felt as though I finally had a claim on my mountain heritage. I was setting tobacco. I was eating fried chicken in my grandmother's kitchen. I was there.

When I think about that meal now, it strikes me that my grandmother intentionally chose to serve the same foods she had always served, especially for Sunday dinner, but in a more convenient way. She made weekly trips to a local grocery store that carried items imported from all over the country and world: she could have served us cold cuts sandwiches, frozen pizzas, or any number of other easy-to-prepare items, but the convenience food she chose was frozen fried chicken, presumably because it was the closest she could get to what she would have served us had she been able to prepare it from scratch. In many ways, that convenience mirrored the change from setting tobacco by hand to doing so by machine and a general shift into modernity, but her food choices also signaled a certain nostalgia for past meals or perhaps for her ability to prepare them.

In researching this project, I became somewhat obsessed with determining what my grandmother would have served at the noonday meal during tobacco season. It seemed to me that, since for many households raising tobacco was an activity in which all family members participated, meals would have needed to be quick and easy to prepare. After years spent hearing my mother lament the physical labor farming life required, it was clear to me that my grandmother likely spent as many hours outside in the fields as she did inside the house. In fact, she preferred to be outside. My mother used to say that my grandmother would rather be "out with the cattle" than inside, dusting the house or sweeping the floor. As anthropologists and oral historians John and Anne van Willigen explain about women in Kentucky between 1920 and 1950, "Most women did both farmwork and food preparation, which meant that they often had to rely on cooking practices that allowed them to spend time in the fields."[2] Time management that fostered calories on the table and plants in the ground was essential.

Historians Rebecca Sharpless and Melissa Walker write about this sometimes difficult negotiation women in the rural South experienced: "Women worked, for the most part, in the places where they lived," meaning that social conventions about the kind of labor deemed appropriate for women at that time were often rendered inconsequential when cash crops like tobacco provided much-needed income.[3] Certainly such was the case for my grandmother. Although she was born into a landowning family that managed to keep and acquire new land during the Depression, she married a tenant farmer and raised three children. They became proud landowners too, but that status was hard-earned and never taken for granted.

Sharpless and Walker point out that the general ideology of the time frowned upon women working in the field for a number of reasons, preferring instead participation in petty-commodity production, like the sale of butter or eggs, which my grandmother also did. They also make clear that working in the field and in the home was demanding at best and damaging at worst, referencing "stories . . . of women working a full day in the blazing sun and still cooking two hot meals, of babies left with siblings who were little more than babies themselves, of damaged uteruses and strained backs."[4] Within a context of such hardship, when I imagine my petite grandmother trying to eke out a living on a mountain farm while being a mother to three children and a wife to an overworked husband, I find it hard to believe that she had much time or energy to plan or make elaborate meals after a morning spent in the field. I find it hard to believe that she was killing, plucking, and frying chickens on a regular basis, even if they could spare the birds. That is not to say that she did not *want* to be creative in the culinary realm—she carefully curated her own homemade cookbook over the course of about twenty years—but the reality of her circumstances made acting upon those culinary inspirations difficult.

Thinking through such things makes me wonder if her choice to serve us Banquet chicken—when her husband had passed away, her children were grown, and cash flowed more freely—was more an act of creating a culinary past she wished had existed than a reflection of the one that actually had: my mother only remembers fried chicken dinners on Sunday, when the family did not work in the field. When I asked her what they ate when setting tobacco, she could not recall the meals with certainty, hypothesizing that maybe my grandmother opened a can of soup or used canned sausage and vegetables she had already prepared. During this conversation my mother paused and admitted, "I don't know what she did. It was hard."

The other problem in determining what my grandmother served during tobacco season is defining "tobacco season." First, specifics about the kind of tobacco grown matter: although bright leaf tobacco, which must be cured using intense heat, was grown in Western North Carolina in the late 1800s, by the time my grandmother was raising tobacco, the variety of choice for Western North Carolinians was burley tobacco, which did not require heat for curing but was instead hung in the barn to air-cure.[5] As retired burley tobacco farmer Jerry Bond told folklorist Ann Ferrell, "Tobacco's commonly known as the 'thirteen-month crop,' because, most times you're still finishing one crop while you're starting the next year's crop—preparing the soil or the seed beds or whatever. You know you may be stripping tobacco, when you're starting the next one."[6] Most families prepared the ground for planting, a process called burning the beds, in either late fall or early spring, followed by planting seeds in spring. Once those seeds matured into plants, the plants were pulled and ready for setting, usually no earlier than mid- to late May. Once the plants were set—the only step in the long process I ever experienced—then they must be cultivated, which involved suckering (the pruning of unhealthy leaves), hoeing, worming, cutting, staking, and hanging to cure in the barn. Most families were not ready to strip their tobacco and arrange it in baskets for sale at market until sometime between late November and mid- to late December, just in time to earn much-anticipated cash for the Christmas holiday.

So my question about what was served at the noonday meal during tobacco season is really asking what my grandmother served midday year-round. Of course, for many families, including my grandmother's, that menu rotated depending on which items were available from the garden. Late spring and summer were replete with fresh vegetables: my mother has fond memories of enjoying new potatoes, fresh lettuces served with hot grease poured over them (an iconic mountain dish called kilt lettuce), and an abundance of tomatoes, squash, cucumbers, and green beans in the summer. Winter meals were more limited, featuring preserved items and less variety. But as retired R. J. Reynolds employee and tobacco variety specialist Carol Miller pointed out to me in conversation, with an influx of cash—what many referred to as "tobacco money"—late December and the month of January were times when families had access to more store-bought goods, including foods not otherwise consumed during the year. It seems reasonable to surmise that by early spring, when tobacco setting took place, most families would have depleted much of their "luxury" food supply purchased with tobacco money. Any Christmas candy or citrus fruits bought to celebrate the holiday season were long gone. After talking with my mother, I was surprised to realize that during the week meat was almost never served, except at breakfast, when fatback was fried to make gravy. At dinner and supper, beans usually provided the protein and were served alongside biscuits or cornbread, milk, and whatever preserved fruits and vegetables my grandmother might have had on hand. I am almost certain fresh fried chicken would not have been on that particular table.

So my question remains: Why did my grandmother choose to serve those items all those years later instead of a more "authentic" meal or another more convenient alternative? I do not think her selections were a gesture at authenticity but rather a conflation of special-occasion meals—ones that featured fried chicken—and an activity that had diminished greatly in acceptability but still took place: by the time I was setting tobacco, people knew that it caused cancer and the tobacco buyouts loomed in the future. To an aging woman who knew that both her time and tobacco's were drawing near, it must have been a comfort to feed us food that was her Sunday best.

It seems safe to say that food commonly evokes feelings of nostalgia for many people, myself included: although I haven't consumed Banquet fried chicken in years, the thought of doing so makes me tear up. Like "authenticity," the word "nostalgia" is a slippery one. Scholar Kimberly Smith explains that Swiss physician Johann Hofer first coined the term in 1688 to describe "Swiss mercenaries who were fighting in foreign lands, defining it as a result of a disturbed imagination, 'a sad mood originating from the desire to return to one's native land.'" Smith goes on to trace the medicalization of the term, particularly as it applied to homesick soldiers and servants, through the nineteenth century. She grapples with evolving definitions of the word, explaining that by the mid-twentieth century the term referenced not a medical condition but instead an emotion: "Once defined as simply a desire to return home, to a specific *place,* nostalgia was gradually being conceptualized as a longing to return to a former *time*—and usually a time the patient only *imagined* to be better." Psychological approaches to the concept varied, including the application of Freudian psychology, and as Smith points out, by 1959 theorists like Charles Zwingmann wrote that nostalgia "is an imagined return to the *past,* rather than to a place."[7] Of course, my grandmother was not a Swiss mercenary longing for home, but I do think she, like many older people, re-created parts of a personal history to soften the sharp edges, offering fried chicken to a granddaughter when the daughter probably ate beans. In other words, I believe the act of serving a more convenient version of fried chicken to loved ones—who were notably participating in the dying tradition of growing tobacco—suggested a brighter version of a remembered past. It was one in which she was able to prepare the meal, had the luxury of doing so despite a number of other demands on her time, and had the financial means to support it.

If my grandmother's lunches of Banquet fried chicken were not, in fact, the marker of authentic mountain heritage I had once believed them to be, then what did that mean for me? Was I forever destined to identify with Hamburger Helper? More broadly, these questions can help us conceptualize the burgeoning popularity of Appalachian cuisine on the national food scene. Appalachian food is, as they say, having a moment, but would my grandmother's lunch of Banquet fried chicken and canned biscuits "count" as mountain? It should, but I am not sure it would.

As pleased as I am that Appalachian food is garnering national praise, it also seems that such veneration sometimes blunts the edges of complex stories. It is difficult to identify when Appalachian food became trendy. In 2005 I took a graduate folklore seminar with Carolyn Ware at Louisiana State University. Although I was enjoying my studies, I was as homesick as a Swiss soldier, so I focused my final project on the cultural significance of ramps.

Though familiar with them, until that semester I had not realized that they were such an important example of Appalachian material culture. When my parents visited me in Baton Rouge that spring, I took them to see the new Whole Foods in town. My father and I were aghast at finding ramps in the produce section for $19.99 a pound. We both stood there, mouths agape, pondering the fact that, first, ramps were for sale in Baton Rouge, a swampland prone to flooding where ramps could never survive; and, second, that someone would be foolish enough to pay $19.99 to purchase the same vegetable my mother banished from our upstairs refrigerator because they made the milk smell bad. Historically, mountain people lauded ramps as a spring tonic essential for cleansing the system and providing the first greens of the year. When a trip to a faraway grocery store to buy out-of-season vegetables was as likely as a flight to the moon, April ramps made a welcome, if smelly, appearance on many mountain tables and at plenty of community suppers. But they also signaled a certain hardscrabble existence within that context, whereas in the Baton Rouge Whole Foods they had come to represent an altogether new kind of cultural capital. The gentrification of ramps had happened, and only the foodiest of the foodies would appreciate their pungent odor, finding it fitting to pay such an exorbitant price to smell rampy for a few days.

Since then ramps have become even more popular, serving as a kind of metaphor for the celebration of mountain food more generally. Three years after the Whole Foods experience, in 2008, longtime Asheville resident, food expert, and cookbook writer Elizabeth Sims organized the "Field to Table Festival: A Taste of Appalachia" at the Biltmore Estate, where chefs and connoisseurs gathered to praise mountain dishes including pickled watermelon and apple stack cake. I had just returned to Western North Carolina when that festival took place and was delighted to know that Appalachian food was being celebrated. By 2011, I began to see chefs like Emeril Lagasse and Bobby Flay using ramps on their cooking shows. That same year I remember reading an issue of the *Wall Street Journal* on an airplane and spying a recipe featuring ramps written by well-known Chapel Hill chef Andrea Reusing. In 2014, award-winning chef and restaurant owner Sean Brock published *Heritage,* a cookbook that highlights his Appalachian roots, and in 2016 food writer Ronni Lundy published *Victuals,* a beautiful cookbook that the *Washington Post* calls "a love letter to Appalachia, with recipes."[8] Other gifted chefs, including Edward Lee, Travis Milton, Ouita Michel, and John Fleer, promote mountain dishes in their restaurants and publications.

Lest we think that this phenomenon of recognizing mountain food is taking place only in the Mountain South, national news stories featuring the trend prove otherwise. On February 27, 2016, the Western North Carolina Blind Pig Supper Club hosted an event called "Appalachian Storytellers" to benefit the Appalachian Food Summit, an organization dedicated to "honor the past, celebrate the present, and support a sustainable future" for Appalachia through food. All 140 tickets sold out in one day. As with all Blind Pig Supper Club events, attendees knew the date and theme of the supper, but not the specific location or menu until just before the event. Participating chefs for the dinner included Travis Milton, Elliott Moss, Mike Moore, Matt Dawes, Ian Boden, and Edward Lee. The event venue, Claxton Farms in Weaverville, North Carolina, was a beautiful and rustic setting for a lively supper featuring dishes ranging from smoked venison to pickled vegetables to leather britches to blackberry dumplings. The event drew plenty of media attention, including that of *Washington Post* reporter Jane Black, who published an article called "The Next Big Thing in American Regional Cooking: Humble Appalachia." Black writes that Appalachian food is "as rich and unexplored in the American culinary scene as Tuscan food was in the 1980s," going on to explain the complexity of food from the Mountain South, noting its Native American roots. Similarly, in January 2017, the Tasting Table website listed "An Appalachian State of Mind" as one of their predictions for "The 9 Most Delicious Food and Drink Trends of the Year."[9]

Certainly such culinary veneration is a welcome shift away from negative stereotypical images of toothless hillbillies who subsist solely on roadkill and moonshine. Although possum and white lightening are stereotypical examples of foods associated with mountain people, they also point to a long history of culinary denigration. Many Appalachian studies scholars agree that the notion of Appalachia as a region distinctly different from the rest of the South and nation began in the years following the Reconstruction. As scholars like Henry Shapiro have pointed out, local color writers, travel writers, and missionaries did much to establish the idea of mountain people as a "strange and peculiar people."[10] Careful examination of these various types of writing produced in the late nineteenth and early twentieth centuries reveals that food was often targeted as a kind of cultural capital in which mountain people were sorely lacking. As one example of many, in local color writer John Fox Jr.'s popular 1903 novel, *The Little Shepherd of Kingdom Come,* a character named Chad boards with a mountain family, and the narrator describes the "coarse food" as "strangely disagreeable."[11] So in many ways it is deeply gratifying to see much-deserved attention being focused on dishes associated with the Mountain South. But I wonder, where in this conversation is my grandmother's story? Is there room at the proverbial table to welcome a woman who killed and fried chicken for some Sunday dinners in the 1950s but also served frozen fried chicken in the 1980s and early '90s not because she loved processed food but because it was as close to "the real thing" as she could get?

Whether or not her story would be welcomed, it is misleading to suggest that everyone agrees on Appalachian food's status as the hottest new food trend. The February/March 2017 edition of *Garden & Gun* magazine, for example, features a story on Nashville-based "Biscuit King" Karl Worley, whose restaurant, Biscuit Love, has become wildly popular. The article highlights Worley's difficult childhood growing up in East Tennessee near Bristol. But it also makes clear that his mountain roots have much to do with his culinary inspiration, citing his grandmother who made biscuits that later inspired his restaurant's feature item. Although Worley values the food traditions from which he came, an odd contradiction appears at the article's conclusion. Author Allison Glock writes about Worley visiting a farmer's market to prepare for an upcoming supper club event in Chattanooga, "the type of high-profile gig he never imagined he'd be part of," going on to state, "Foodieville is a far cry from Appalachia, where [Worley says] 'we'd live on beans and cornbread for a month.'"[12] A few dynamics are at play here: First, Chattanooga is by all accounts part of the Appalachian region,[13] and thus the kind of high-end food Glock imagines to be served at the supper club is also Appalachian; it is not an anomaly but rather part of the diverse culinary spectrum available in the mountains. Second, it remains unclear whether Worley shares Glock's opinion that "Foodieville is a far cry from Appalachia"—her words, not his. In this instance, beans and cornbread are framed as foods of culinary deprivation related as much to class as they are to region. Such focus highlights Worley's success since he was able to "rise above" the background from which he came. The general tone of the article, especially its conclusion, signals that not all food writers take part in the veneration of long-derided foods, instead using them as a counterpoint to haute cuisine.

Even so, the celebration of mountain foods is happening on a large scale, and we need to be careful in how we go about celebrating a long-undervalued cuisine and people. In 2015, foodways scholar Elizabeth Engelhardt wrote that "Appalachia is poised to be the next big thing in food circles," and it seems as though that time has come. She warns that we may inadvertently fetishize mountain food in the same way that southern food has been idolized.[14] The unfortunate result of such wide-reaching veneration is that it dulls the edge of complex food stories, ones that consider race, class, geographic differences, and so much more.

Food writers, chefs, scholars, and community activists are aware of these dangers and are working to avoid them. The Appalachian Food Summit, for example, has hosted several annual events. The 2016 summit in Berea, Kentucky, based its theme on rivers and routes in Appalachia, highlighting diverse culinary paths in the region. Food writer Courtney Balestier spoke about the

Italian roots of the pepperoni roll in West Virginia, while rhetoric and composition professor Steven Alvarez explained how his University of Kentucky class on "taco literacy" encourages students to learn about Mexican migration in the state. Efforts such as these are precisely what Engelhardt called for in 2015 and what I fear we may not have enough of. For example, Jane Black's review of *Victuals,* while beautifully written and a positive take on Ronni Lundy's book, also prompted one reader to respond:

> How delightful that you assume that ALL West Virginians
> are bean experts, or that we ALL savor ramps or any of the
> other Appalachian delicacies. I grew up in North Central
> West Virginia, where the number of immigrants from
> Italy, Poland, the Ukraine, etc. outnumber people [traditionally considered] . . . "Appalachian." While the latter has
> a distinct and proud heritage, I can tell you for a fact that
> people like me never ate that type of food, and I myself had
> never even heard of most of it until I grew up and travelled throughout the rest of the state. Our . . . childhood
> favorites include the foods that our grandparents and
> parents kept as authentic: cabbage rolls, pierogis, kielbasa,
> spaghetti, gnocchi, lasagna, pizza, and most importantly,
> the snack invented in Fairmont, WV, the pepperoni roll.[15]

This reader's disdain is palpable and points to an often overlooked pitfall of celebrating a food and people that has long been criticized: doing so can be essentializing, suggesting that a fairly narrow menu of items could represent an entire region and its people, when in fact, it cannot. In upholding particular foods like leather britches, creasy greens, ramps, poke sallet, pickled watermelon, apple stack cake, and a number of other iconic mountain foods, other foods do not seem to qualify, even if mountain people ate, or still eat, them.

There are also problematic racial overtones implied in the foods that writers typically highlight when discussing Appalachia, revealing an implicit—and often inaccurate—understanding that these foods originated with people of Scots-Irish descent. The consequence is that the rich ethnic history of many foods is left unexplored: not all Appalachians were or are Scots-Irish, and neither is their food. As writers like Ronni Lundy and many others have worked hard to explain, these food traditions have a vast history ranging from Africa to Germany to precolonial America. Celebrating foods without understanding where they came from can be just as damaging as perpetuating stereotypes of ignorant hillbillies.

Cultivating a narrow definition of what "counts" as mountain food is dangerous territory as well. Although it pleases me to no end to be able to order leather britches at a high-end restaurant or eat ramps in New York City, I am also keenly aware that the majority of farmers I know who live in Western North Carolina could not afford to eat in those restaurants; the same is true for many people in other occupations. Moreover, given the demands placed on people's time in a difficult economy, especially in parts of Appalachia dependent on coal, it also seems unlikely that many people have the time or ability to cook what we have come to understand as "traditional" mountain foods. I am privileged in a number of ways, yet I know that during most weeks I cannot find the time to make an apple stack cake. Like my grandmother and her fried chicken, I would buy a frozen version if I could find one. I would happily serve it to my family if they were helping me set tobacco.

This is not to suggest that no one enjoys suppers of beans and cornbread anymore: of course they do. But we should take note that although the "coarse" food of the mountains has been redeemed, the cultural shaming that equated so-called inferior foods with mountain people in the late nineteenth and early to mid-twentieth centuries still occurs today. In other words, the recipe is the same, but the ingredients have changed: now mountain people are frequently associated with processed foods. In 2009, for example, Diane Sawyer hosted the 20/20 special "A Hidden America: Children of the Mountains" in which she calls Appalachia "a world apart," where there is a "documented epidemic of . . . toothlessness" due in part to what many people call "Mountain Dew Mouth."

Sawyer's condescending tone indicates a clear bias against people who would reportedly put Mountain Dew in a baby's bottle or consume so much of the sugary soda that they ruin their teeth. But her coverage of this disturbing issue neglects to mention the point made by NPR journalist Eliza Barclay in a 2013 article after speaking with Priscilla Harris, an associate professor at the Appalachian College of Law who was researching the problem: "Many people don't trust the well water in their homes because of pollution concerns and probably drink more soda because of it." So rather than suggesting that sheer ignorance or negligence lies at the root of so much soda consumption, it might instead be that polluted drinking water—likely the result of poorly regulated mining practices—is at least partly to blame. Barclay also cites cultural reasons for the drink's popularity, claiming that the region has a "distinct culture of sipping soda constantly throughout the day." Perhaps that might be true, but isn't that also true for many Americans? According to a recent report published by the Centers for Disease Control, "50.6% of U.S. adults consumed at least one SSB [sugar-sweetened beverage] on a given day." And on January 26, 2017, the *Washington Post* website published an article lamenting the fact that although for the past several years Americans were drinking less soda, that declining trend has stopped. The article quotes nutrition professor and spokeswoman for the American Heart Association Rachel Johnson: "We recommend that children drink soda once a week or less. We're seeing that two-thirds drink it on a daily basis."[16] So while mountain people may prefer Mountain Dew over another sugary soda, as with many social ills attributed to Appalachia, this one seems endemic to our contemporary American culture, not just the mountains.

Yet the impulse to connect Appalachian people with processed foods and to denigrate them for it persists. In the spring 2015 issue of *Oxford American,* Chris Offutt, born and raised in eastern Kentucky, published an essay called "Trash Food." In it, he recounts the invitation he received from acclaimed food scholar and writer John T. Edge to give a talk about "trash food" at the next Southern

Foodways Alliance symposium. Offutt describes his initial dis-
comfort on hearing the request, going on to explain the current
trend of "'white trash parties' where people are urged to bring
Cheetos, pork rinds, Vienna sausages, Jell-O with marshmallows,
fried baloney, corndogs, RC Cola, Slim Jims, Fritos, Twinkies, and
cottage cheese with jelly. In short—the food [Offutt] ate as a kid in
the hills." Had Offutt been living a century earlier, his list would
have no doubt included the very items that are now served at Blind
Pig suppers and written about in the *Washington Post*. He explains,
"The term 'trash food' is not about food, it's coded language for
social class. It's about poor people and what they can afford to eat."[17]
So while it may be trendy now to pay big bucks for ramps at Whole
Foods and eat leather britches at fund-raising suppers—I attend
those suppers when I can and enjoy them very much—we need to
keep in mind that just because we are finally celebrating food that
deserves long-overdue recognition, the hurtful paradigm of culinary cultural shaming that connects region with class endures.

If anything, processed food like Banquet frozen fried chicken
allowed my grandmother an opportunity to share a rich, valuable
culinary heritage with me that she otherwise would not have had.
By the time I was helping her set tobacco, she was not able to tend a
stove, let alone butcher a chicken. Yet despite the culinary memory
Banquet frozen fried chicken afforded me, it is hard to glorify the
industrial practices that likely contributed to its production. Like
so many conveniences, her access to that chicken almost certainly
came at a cost to someone else. Historian Bryant Simon explains
that "in 1987, chicken cost the same in real dollars as it had in 1923,"
meaning that those involved in getting the chickens to market,
processed, and on the shelves were frequently exploited.[18] Farmers and chicken plant workers were especially vulnerable. In one
fatal example of poor labor practices, on September 3, 1991, a fire
broke out at the Imperial Food Products chicken plant in Hamlet,
North Carolina, killing twenty-five workers because building exits
were blocked or locked. It was a revelation to me that the Hamlet fire occurred in 1991, almost certainly a year that I helped my

grandmother set tobacco. Writing this essay has highlighted for me a variety of ways to think about that chicken: as the centerpiece of a treasured family memory; as a vehicle for my grandmother's cultural expression and an opportunity to transform store-bought, processed food into a mountain feast; as potential fodder for those eager to connect processed foods with regional identity and, in turn, inferior cultural standing; and finally, as an edible reminder of America's insistence on cheap food, no matter the human cost.

All this theorizing and soapboxing leaves me with more questions than answers, but I do know that you don't get more mountain than my grandmother: her family has been in Western North Carolina for well over two hundred years and her maiden name, Ramsey, is as familiar in her home county of Madison as the surname Smith is to the American population. While I am not advocating that chefs like John Fleer start serving Banquet chicken at their restaurants, I am suggesting that we think carefully about culinary exoneration and the forms it takes. In many ways, it seems as though the contemporary craze over mountain food—which again, I am *glad* is happening—runs the risk of doing the same kind of romanticizing I was indulging in when I imagined my grandmother preparing elaborate lunches to serve during tobacco setting. Although those lunches may have happened occasionally, they were not the norm. Likewise, although apple stack cake is a treasured mountain dessert worth celebrating, it is labor-intensive and calls for a variety of ingredients, including imported items like cinnamon. Many mountain bakers would not have had the time or resources to make the dish on a regular basis, thus reserving it for special occasions. Such context does not diminish the importance of the dish but rather serves as an important reminder not to be swept away in creating an image of the past that probably never existed in reality.

Instead, an inclusive approach that explores the nuances of memory, food, and nostalgia seems more fitting. Returning to Kimberly Smith's discussion of nostalgia can also help us understand why the impulse might be so strong to uplift mountain food, no matter how generalized the definition. She explains that when the concept of nostalgia was first defined, it had a clear medical connotation and was believed to affect "dislocated rural people." She goes on to explain: "It was a distinctive symptom of the social dislocation that was the hallmark of industrialization: the movement from rural agriculture to urban factories and commerce."[19] Certainly mountain people know something about leaving home to find industrial work: in the twentieth century, scores of Appalachians migrated to coal mining towns and mill towns in search of jobs.[20] Appalachian authors like Ron Rash imagine what that transition must have felt like; much of his poetry explores the painful relationship rural people have with their homes after leaving them. His collection *Eureka Mill*, for example, features poems that chronicle the experience of transitioning from a farm-based economy to one that relies on work in textile mills for income. In the poem "Spring Fever," the speaker describes mill workers who long for life on the farm, especially during the spring planting season. But the speaker reasons that the men are "just remembering the best" and "It's easy to love a life / you only have to live the good parts of."[21] For me, I cannot remember "the best" since I did not grow up farming in the first place. Consequently, I cherish the few connections I have to the agrarian existence that sustained previous generations in my family. While that sentimental attachment is understandable, it also led me to romanticize my grandmother's experience in ways that I later realized were not true to her reality. Only she could tell me what she served while setting tobacco, and sadly, she is no longer here for me to ask.

Our contemporary focus on mountain cuisine risks romanticizing a culture the same way I did with my grandmother. In a postmodern, global world, it can feel comforting to isolate a certain set of foods to one region, to identify with them culturally, and to celebrate them. I do not question or criticize that impulse. For many overworked people in the twenty-first century, although we often live a lifestyle that privileges convenience foods over more labor-intensive methods that yield tastier results, the foods we dream of are often the ones we do not have time to prepare. I have a robust collection of "when I find the time" recipes that grows with every passing year. Yet I also believe that an honest look at the foods mountain people ate and eat today will provide a much clearer window through which to investigate the reality of the Appalachian region, as well as opportunities to question the production practices of what we eat. We need to be aware of whose stories and whose foods we omit. It makes sense that frozen, processed food, like my grandmother's Banquet chicken, would be viewed as the food item we are trying *not* to remember. But we should.

NOTES

1. Fitzhugh Brundage, "From Appalachian Folk to Southern Foodways: Why Americans Look to the South for Authentic Culture," in *Creating and Consuming the American South*, ed. Martyn Bone, Brian Ward, and William A. Link (Gainesville: University Press of Florida, 2015), 29–30.

2. John van Willigen and Anne van Willigen, *Food and Everyday Life on Kentucky Family Farms, 1920–1950*, Kentucky Remembered: An Oral History Series (Lexington: University Press of Kentucky, 2006), 13.

3. Rebecca Sharpless and Melissa Walker, "'Pretty Near Every Woman Done a Man's Work': Women and Field Work in the Rural South," in *Work, Family, and Faith: Rural Southern Women in the Twentieth Century*, ed. Melissa Walker and Rebecca Sharpless (Columbia: University of Missouri Press, 2006), 43.

4. Sharpless and Walker, "'Pretty Near Every Woman,'" 49–50.

5. Tom Lee, "Southern Appalachia's Nineteenth-Century Bright Tobacco Boom: Industrialization, Urbanization, and the Culture of Tobacco," *Agricultural History* 88, no. 2 (Spring 2014): 175–206.

6. Ann K. Ferrell, *Burley: Kentucky Tobacco in a New Century*, Kentucky Remembered: An Oral History Series (Lexington: University Press of Kentucky, 2013), 40.

7. Kimberly K. Smith, "Mere Nostalgia: Notes on a Progressive Paratheory," *Rhetoric and Public Affairs* 3, no. 4 (2000): 509–13.

8. Andrea Reusing, "Asparagus and Ramp Skillet Soufflé," *Wall Street Journal*, May 28, 2011, sec. Cooking & Eating. Sean Brock, *Heritage* (New York: Artisan, 2014); Ronni Lundy, *Victuals: An Appalachian Journey, with Recipes* (New York: Clarkson Potter, 2016). Jane Black,

"'Victuals,' Reviewed: A Love Letter to Appalachia, with Recipes," *Washington Post*, August 30, 2016.

9. For more on the Blind Pig Supper Club, see "Who We Are," http://theblindpigsupperclub.com/gallery/. On the Appalachian Food Summit, see "What We Do," https://www.appalachianfood.com/what-we-do. Jane Black, "The Next Big Thing in American Regional Cooking: Humble Appalachia," *Washington Post*, March 29, 2016. Team Tasting Table, "Back to the Future: Our Predictions for the 9 Most Delicious Food and Drink Trends of the Year," *Tasting Table*, January 4, 2017, https://www.tastingtable.com/dine/national/best-food-drink-trends -2017.

10. Henry D. Shapiro, *Appalachia on Our Mind: The Southern Mountains and Mountaineers in the American Consciousness, 1870–1920* (Chapel Hill: University of North Carolina Press, 1978); Will Wallace Harney, "A Strange Land and a Peculiar People," *Lippincott's Magazine* 12, no. 31 (October 1873): 429–38.

11. John Fox, Jr., *The Little Shepherd of Kingdom Come* (New York: Grosset & Dunlap, 1903), 153.

12. Allison Glock, "The Biscuit King," *Garden & Gun*, February/March 2017, 113.

13. Culturally speaking, Chattanooga shares much with other parts of Appalachia, and it is in Hamilton County, which the Appalachian Regional Commission lists as an Appalachian county. See Appalachian Regional Commission, "Counties in Appalachia," https://www.arc.gov /appalachian_region/CountiesinAppalachia.asp.

14. Elizabeth S. D. Engelhardt, "Appalachian Chicken and Waffles: Countering Southern Food Fetishism," *Southern Cultures* 21, no. 1 (2015): 78, doi:10.1353/scu.2015.0003.

15. Black, "'Victuals,' reviewed."

16. Eliza Barclay, "'Mountain Dew Mouth' Is Destroying Appalachia's Teeth, Critics Say," *NPR.org*, September 19, 2013, http://www.npr. org/sections/thesalt/2013/09/12/221845853/mountain-dew-mouth-is -destroying-appalachias-teeth. Sohyun Park et al., "Prevalence of Sugar-Sweetened Beverage Intake among Adults—23 States and the District of Columbia, 2013," *MMWR: Morbidity and Mortality Weekly Report* 65, no. 7 (2016): 169, doi:10.15585/mmwr.mm6507a1. Caitlin Dewey, "Americans Were Making a Lot of Progress Cutting Back on Sugary Drinks. Now That's Stopped," *Washington Post*, January 26, 2017.

17. Chris Offutt, "Trash Food," *Oxford American* 88 (Spring 2015): 126.

18. Bryant Simon, *The Hamlet Fire: A Tragic Story of Cheap Food, Cheap Government, and Cheap Lives* (New York: New Press, 2017), 78.

19. Smith, "Mere Nostalgia," 511.

20. For more information about this shift, see Chad Berry, *Southern Migrants, Northern Exiles* (Urbana: University of Illinois Press, 2000); Ronald D. Eller, *Miners, Millhands, and Mountaineers: Industrialization of the Appalachian South, 1880–1930*, 1st ed., Twentieth-Century America Series (Knoxville: University of Tennessee Press, 1982).

21. Ron Rash, *Eureka Mill* (Columbia, SC: Bench Press, 1998), 17.

Chapter 3

Gardens of Eden

Karida L. Brown

I CAN'T say that foodways in the African American enclaves of eastern Kentucky were any different than in other Black communities throughout the United States during the mid-twentieth century. This is because, in the end, we Black folks were all drawing from a similar set of traditions; traveling with the embodied stories of places and practices that our ancestors cultivated during our country's centuries-long commitment to racial slavery and segregation. Up until 1910, 90 percent of the Black population in the United States still resided in the American South. Therefore, although our beautiful branches, blossoms, and leaves spread out all over the country, most of our roots run deep back through the rich red soil of the South. This is conveyed through all manner of cultural expression, including our food.

For this reason, kitchens of African American families during the Jim Crow and civil rights eras tell tales of racialized and gendered labor, migration, survival, struggle, striving, celebration, culture, and love. You will find that daddies know how to kill a hog and use its products from the roota to the toota, mamas can catch and kill a chicken with one hand and in one fell swoop, and grandparents can tell by the taste in the air at spring's eve whether it's going to be a good season for this or that crop. In this essay, I illuminate these intersections between race, region, gender, generation, and food by way of the collective memory of a generation of African Americans whose roots run deep through the Appalachian region of eastern Kentucky. What follows is a retelling of the stories and experiences of the coal camp Blacks who hail from Harlan County, Kentucky. These Black folks represent the children of the generation of coal miners and homemakers who lived and worked in the Kentucky towns of Benham, Cumberland, and Lynch during the first half of the twentieth century. Although these former company-owned towns are now mere remnants of what they were during the coal boom, they very much live on in the collective memory of the coal miners' sons and daughters who share eastern Kentucky roots.[1] Our portal of entry in this analysis is a place that I am sure is near and dear to many readers: the garden.

"EVERYBODY HAD A GARDEN"

Everybody's daddy was a coal miner and everybody's mama was a homemaker. At the same time, mama, daddy, and child worked a family garden. African American families brought this agricultural tradition with them on their migration from plantations where so many of them sharecropped in Alabama to coalfields of eastern Kentucky. In this mass migration from the Deep South to central Appalachia, they brought with them what few worldly possessions they owned; their hopes, dreams, and aspirations; their work ethic; and their traditions. By virtue of landing jobs with the mining companies, United States Steel Corporation, and International Harvester, this generation of African Americans transformed from "peasant to proletariat";[2] from subsistence agricultural workers who mainly survived off the land and through barter, to wage earners in an industrial labor economy. However, despite this shift in their relationship to labor, these families did not trust that they could rely on a company salary to feed their large families. Such trust would be of little consequence in any case, for agriculture was a part of who they were. In eastern Kentucky, gardening provided a stable food source for families and the community in times of plenty and in times of flux.

During the first half of the twentieth century, the men worked as coal miners for International Harvester and United States Steel Corporation. The work was long and grueling, as it required them to risk their lives going into and under a mountain to manually extract that bituminous coal. It was the coal companies that put a roof over their heads, but too often, it was their gardens that put food on the table. Because of their ties to the Deep South, they had an intimate knowledge of agricultural science—of the soil, the weather, crops, and raising farm animals.

So what's in a garden? Yes, it's obviously a source of produce. But it was so much more than that to these folks. For them, the garden was a site of intergenerational knowledge transmission and a family structure that instilled work ethic and reified gender roles. It was also a place of play and folly, one that generated some of the fondest memories that my own parents, and many of their childhood friends, have to look back on when they think about home.

Well, that's another thing. Everybody in Lynch had a garden, okay. A garden now is almost like the in thing to do, but back then it was a necessity. It was just part of everybody's lifestyle that supplemented whatever food that you bought from the store with fresh everything. So we helped in the garden, and we had a lot of what they call "vegetarian meals" now—meatless meals like pinto beans, greens, corn bread; that was the meal with tomatoes and cucumbers and onions. *(Wanda Davis)*

Well at that time, growing up in Lynch, my dad would come home from work and he would make us go up on the hill. So many men, they would pick them up a spot on the side of the mountain and we would dig it up and make a garden. *(George Massey)*

Yes, we raised chickens on the hillside where we just lived. Everybody in the community had a garden and in their yard they raised their own greens, beans, tomatoes and then like chickens, like livestock didn't too much live in your yard, you know they didn't raise them in your yard because they had them on the hillside. Everybody had a place for their own livestock; you know to feed the chickens. *(Sanford Baskin)*

Oh a huge garden! My father raised all kinds of vegetables: corn, cucumbers, tomatoes, squash, he was pretty green thumbed. He could really raise a garden, and he had us out there helping him work it, to keep it weeded and stuff. So even though we were poor as children we didn't know that we were poor, because we always had something to eat, he always provided and he always made sure that his animals had it. *(Raveryn Whit)*

It was as though the men had two full-time jobs: working in the mines, and working in their gardens. And these were not your small leisurely plots. No, these were huge gardens carved out of the mountainside; ones that were made to bear enough food to support a family of eight, ten, or sometimes up to sixteen children. The garden was a source of food and sustainability for the family. It was a site of shared labor and collective responsibility, and a space where gender, family, and generational roles were calcified.

Everybody had a job, everyone had a role. The boys were with Dad to do the garden but with girls we did the dishes and of course making our beds when they really got on us to make the beds. *(Sally Pettygrue)*

And the ladies in the [coal] camps, they would do a lot of canning, and they would can the vegetables and things and put them away, you know and you could eat on those, you know during the winter months when there was no garden. And one thing we did, we ate good. *(Clara Smith)*

My mother would can; she would do jelly, she would do green beans and tomatoes. She would make this apple butter. She would make applesauce. *(Betty Williams)*

And we used to peel a lot of peaches and apples and bake beans and greens, wash and all of that. And all these stuff went in the jar and then they had this big number three tub that you put over fire. We'd have stuff cooking all night in the jars for canning. *(Arletta Andrews)*

As we can see, the garden served as a sorting ground for shaping gender roles. Mothers and their daughters cleaned, canned, and preserved the bounty of that season's harvest, while the fathers and their sons worked the land.

Oh Lord, I used to hate to go up there. We used to have to go up there and weed it out. Get all those weeds out and it would be in the heat of the day. You come home from school thinking you would be able to go and play, no, you had to go to the garden. You had to go to garden, and your dad would show you how to cut around the plants and not to cut them up and mound the dirt up around them round all your plants. And where the water would soak and keep the roots good and damp. Man, I used to hate that. *(George Massey)*

Daddy would take Thornton and Mike and Ken up there; that's why Thornton doesn't have a garden to this day: Daddy worn him out! And he would weed and everything was just so good. *(Patricia Joanne Davis Liggins)*

My grandfather had sheep, goats, cows, hogs, and then the hogs would have little kids and sometimes they had the tendency to get out a little. We as kids wanted them to get out so we could chase them down and everything and catch them. And we milked the goats and this may sound funny to you but at that time people that had ulcers, they say that goat milk was good for ulcers, so we would milk the goat and we get the milk and there was a white man that had ulcers and we sold that milk for fifty cents or something like that and my grandfather would let us keep that fifty cents. And we would make butter from the goat milk and butter from cow milk. . . . Now this may sound funny to you, when we were kids we had to milk the cow but now if a cow had a small kid she would have the tendency to pour her milk back and what we would do then as kids, young boys, we would take and skeet the milk inside each other's mouths and faces. *(Ernest Pettygrue)*

These families worked hard, and they enjoyed the fruits of their labor. They didn't think anything of it because it was a way of life back then, but in retrospect many of these coal miners' children joked that they had "whole foods before there was a Whole Foods." They did not rely on the produce sold at the company store. Instead, like the premise upon which so many restaurants pride themselves today, they were accustomed to garden to table meals. Not only did they eat fresh, they all played a role in cultivating the garden and producing the food. Unlike so many children today, they knew exactly where their food came from. In the months that did not bear a crop, they relied on the produce that their mothers had canned the fall before.

Yes, it was fresh food. I was very young when she used
to can them but I actually remember the beautiful sight
of vegetable and the fruits. She had a way of doing it and
when you take it out it's not really soft like [canned food].
It was so good, Karida. It was so delicious. *(Patricia Brown)*

Fresh food, you know we didn't go to the stores. *(Sanford Baskin)*

She cooked a lot, and we ate out of our garden and we just
didn't realize that we were eating good food. Like greens
coming out of the garden; tomatoes, sweet potatoes, corn;
all of that came out of the garden. We had Whole Foods
and we did not realize that we were eating good food.
And she would make pound cakes and one of her favorite
things that she would make during the week is these tea-
cakes and they were so good. *(Vyreda Davis Williams)*

ONE feature of a coal town was that the company owned everything. The company owned all the housing stock, the stores where
their employees would spend their hard-earned dollars or compa-
ny-issued scrip, the schools, the churches, and the land. Families
were eligible to live in the company-owned coal town only if the
man of the house was employed by the company. This socially en-
gineered community structure created an artificial labor economy,
in which a miner's salary could suffice to support a large family.
Coal companies had an incentive to create environments where
stable family structures could flourish in order to insure a steady
workforce. Therefore, unlike most African American women
living in industrial cities at the time, few wives and mothers in
the Tri-cities area of Harlan County worked outside the home. It
was deemed far more valuable to encourage hyper-gendered labor
roles, where fathers worked in the mines and mothers tended to
all home affairs. Therefore, as you can imagine, these were some

cooking mothers. So what was on the table in these Black Appalachian households?

> Well, in the morning time for breakfast, we would have homemade biscuits, we would have rice, breads, we would have eggs and bacon, ham or whatever. Coffee, tea, milk, really had anything just about anything that we wanted. Fruit and stuff like that. And for lunch, that would fix our lunch and we would take it to school with us. We had some sandwiches and some fruits, and everything in the dessert. And they made dessert every day—I always had dessert at supper. And for supper, we would have, we would have some beans, some greens, rice and different sorts of things, you know, different vegetables: collard greens, turnip greens, mustards. *(Lena Margaret Jones)*

> We had homemade biscuits, we had rice, pork chop, gravy and that was our Sunday morning breakfast. *(Vera Robinson)*

> And Sundays were big-time dinners so everybody would stop at our house. If you lived in Lynch and you walked the streets of Lynch, you knew Mrs. Pumpkin would always cook big pans of rolls. If nothing else Mrs. Pumpkin would get you a couple of rolls and everybody knew she could cook the best cakes. And her chicken and dressing and dumplings and her potato salad was to die for. *(Jeff Turner)*

> Well, Sunday was the big meal. You always had homemade rolls, fried chicken, macaroni and cheese, greens or green beans, you always had a cake and some ice cream. That was given on a Sunday. Saturday you may have had hot dogs and French fries, that was like that day the kids enjoy the most because it was you know just junk type food. But during the week it was always a meal when you came home from school. You always have something you know greens, beans, neck bones you know some kind of

meat you had a warm meal that everybody sat around the table around 4:00 and Mother said dinner is ready. And that's how we grew up you know a meal every day. There just wasn't a day the children didn't have a cooked meal and if for some reason you didn't want that meal, my parents being that my daddy farmed had all kinds of foods—potatoes, he would—they would allow us to you know cook French fries after you cleaned up the kitchen and cook so you have something extra. Maybe you didn't want this homemade soup that mother had made so you could cook French fries and toast and hot chocolate. So you know we always had food. We had every vegetable because my father you know had his garden from tomatoes to beans to corn to popcorn. (Arnita Davis Brown)

And Mama used quite a few eggs because she made the bread—you didn't see nobody buying no breads. And she would make a cornbread for supper and biscuit bread for all of the other meals. In the morning she made the biscuit, evening she made the cornbread and that was seven days a week. (Odell Moss)

Well, my mum, bless her heart, she would get up; I could hear her down in the kitchen. And she would be humming and singing gospel songs and I would get up. And at the time the boys slept on this side and the girls slept on this side of the house. And they had a vent in the floor just like these squares here, but they weren't all the way up, it was over the top of the warm morning stove. That is where the heat would come up and heat the room. And also when she was down there cooking, that aroma would come up through there. And we had to get up and go down there and she would beat—like the night before, she had beat and made up a big bowl of dough bread. And she would get up that morning and roll it out and make biscuits and we—I would never forget; we had killed some hogs and Dad had a like a meat house under the house. And he would put this meat in there and salt it down, let it cure. And it wasn't nothing to go out there and get a big slab of bacon. They cut it and put it in that skillet and oh man. You talk about smelling good, oh man! *(George Massey)*

THE outdoors was a garden too. Nestled in the valleys of the sprawling eastern Kentucky mountains, these children had an abundance of riches when it came to wild produce. The mountains were a veritable "Garden of Eden." Wild fruit grew all over the place. As children, my parents' generation would start their weekend mornings off with a hike up the mountain to go fruit picking. Blackberries, apples, peaches, walnuts—the mountainscape was bursting with bounty.

> There were a lot of trees. The good Lord provided everything; he really did. Because we could go three or four miles into the mountains; we would find all type of apple trees, blackberries, blueberries. . . . We would find all that stuff in the woods in the mountains, and the good Lord provided all that stuff. *(Jack French)*

> Wild fruit was all over the place; just walk out of your backyard right up on the hill there and there they were. They were all in different places, and when you go blackberry picking in the morning you would see a lot of your buddies, "Hey I'll see you later man!"; everybody would go different ways. We would have sacks if we were going to do apples, or we would have these big buckets if we were going to pick the blackberries; and that is how we did it. Same thing with hunting; my dad taught us and brought me into hunting with a little .22 rifle, and we used to kill squirrels and groundhogs. And take them home, skin them, cook them up. Rabbits, the whole thing, and fishing, we would do a lot of fishing. *(William Jackson)*

On one mountain there was a wild apple orchard and we would take a cloth sack up on the mountain and fill it with apples and roll it down. We would also walk along the railroad tracks and pick wild strawberries and those kinds of things; we would bring them home; or Mother would can them. We also had hogs up on the mountain; I never saw them because the girls wouldn't go up there; my brothers had to feed them. (Harriett Hillie)

And we would pick blackberries. And we would pick buckets of them all over the mountain. They would just grow wild. Big whole berries; some that big. Big ol' beautiful berries. (George Massey)

Oh yes, we used to go blackberry picking; we used to go and get all the nuts. We used to go and get wild grapes, we called them possum grapes. We used to go and get those grapes and go up in the mountains and go and pick apples, and then we used to go up in the mountains sometimes just to play. There would be vines up there, and we would swing on the vines and we would tie them onto tree ends and then we would go up there and you know . . . (Victor Prinkleton)

The bounty of the land was a source of petty cash for the children in the community. They could always count on the adults in the neighborhood to support their endeavors.

We would pick blackberries and you could pick a gallon of blackberries and they would give you twenty-five cents for that gallon that you done picked all that time, and even if you got twenty-five cents you thought you had something back then. (Ernest Pettygrue)

They paid us for it. I'd get me a chili dog, yes and go to the fountain, you know go somewhere and buy me an ice-cream, popsicle, go to our little local stores we had around and buy me a handful of bubble gum. Yes we made money like, that little money that we made was a lot of money. *(Sanford Baskin)*

I would go up in the mountains and we would stay all day sometimes. But during summer we would go up there and pick blackberries. And I would take some home and sell them. And you could always sell blackberries, really. They were very easy to sell because you know a lot of women, you know baked pies and that type of thing. *(Edwin Gist)*

The garden also was a place of community, childhood folly, and mischief. It's funny how families knew each other by their gardens. Whose garden had what, who you could steal from, who would shoot you. It was another way of relating.

And we was little thieves back then, because we'd steal the corn grains; the tomatoes would be out there. We'd get back there and we'd sit and eat the corn; because it'd be so good. *(Katina Akal)*

We used to take our saltshakers with us and go up to Mr. Johnny's garden to steal some of his tomatoes. I don't know a kid who didn't. *(Cynthia Brown Harrington)*

I wouldn't trade those years for anything in the world. It was just so fulfilling, so much fun. We had opportunities just to be boys. We did everything that boys do. Picked blackberries, picked apples, built scooters, rolled tires, played marbles, fight and make up and fight again. And we'd get into our fair share of trouble like getting into someone's grapevine and getting the grapes at night until they found out and tell our parents, and going into someone's yard and getting apples from the tree without permission. *(P. G. Peeples)*

And Mr. Johnny Pettygrue had the biggest garden around here. And everybody knew his garden. We'd go there and sit down and eat them tomatoes all day long. And he would let you go sit! He planted enough so that the thieves could get some, you know, he had enough for everybody, I am telling you. It wasn't like you had to ask nobody for nothing. *(Roy Stevens)*

BLACK MOUNTAIN KIDS

These are the childhood memories of the Black kids who grew up at the foot of Black Mountain in Harlan County, Kentucky. Perhaps their stories brought you back to your own memories in the mountains. There is nothing exclusively Black about their experiences—save for old Jim Crow drawing the contours of their cultural geographies. The inherent irony that lies within the montage of stories and memories presented in this essay, however, is its taste. This is a sweet sweet story about a generation of carefree Black children who happened to grow up in one of the most historically contested places in American labor history, and at the same time under the auspices of Jim Crow—one of the most violent racial institutions since emancipation. How can it be that they experienced such a halcyon life under those dual oppressive structures? Or at least, how could these people remember it in such a way? I point to three factors that help explain how these stark contradictions persisted, yet still allowed for experiences and memories that seem so fond.

International Harvester and U.S. Steel Corporation established Benham and Lynch as "model towns." An effort in social engineering, model towns were envisioned as corporate utopias by which a company would supply all of its employees' needs and most of their wants in exchange for hard work and blind obedience. This was largely an effort to thwart unionization efforts rampant throughout coal country at the time. As a result, families of all races and ethnicities in these towns lived lives of comfort and stability relative to other coal towns in the region. The homes were well maintained, with running water and plumbing. The companies operated top-notch private school systems (although they were segregated), and further, they offered decent wages, universal health care, and other forms of social welfare that provided this population a level of stability and prosperity that was unusual for eastern Kentucky company-owned towns at that time. This is not to say that everyone was well off, or even thriving. What it did mean, however, is that the company actively intervened on behalf of its employees to create a safety net for miners and their families.

A second point in this regard is that deprivation is relative. As my research participants often state, "We may have been poor, but we didn't know it!" This is because in a company-owned town, there is little variation in families' socioeconomic status. In this way, whether or not they were deprived, they did not *feel* it.

A third point worth highlighting is that this is just as much a story about Jim Crow segregation as it is about Appalachian foodways. The African American families in eastern Kentucky lived in close-knit, hermetically sealed Black communities not by choice, but by force. Jim Crow was the law of the land and of public opinion, and it was all that these children and their parents had ever known. As a result, this generation of African Americans was not inclined to look to the state, their employer, or white fellow Americans to ensure their family's safety or well-being. While gardening, raising livestock, bartering among neighbors, and canning generated a great sense of community and nostalgia in this population of African Americans, these were by no means the underlying motivations for action. It was instead a matter of survival.

As their stories show, although the children of this generation were raised in Appalachia, the community's food traditions can be traced back to their parents' and grandparents' roots in the Deep South—to those practices and recipes that emerged out of a time and context that no longer exist. Those Black parents brought with them the will and know-how to make do. These coalmining families may not have been rich in material things, but they had it all.

I can't remember any time we had no food in the house. There were some times when it wasn't what you wanted, but there was always something to eat. That's why I said that my dad and mom were great. We might have been short, but never hungry. There was always something to eat—may not be what you wanted to eat, but there was always something to eat. *(Richard Brown)*

NOTES

1. All interviews quoted here are drawn from my larger Eastern Kentucky African American Migration Project (EKAAMP), in collaboration with the Southern Historical Collection at University of North Carolina at Chapel Hill, http://ekaamp.web.unc.edu. See also Karida L. Brown, *Gone Home: Race and Roots through Appalachia* (Chapel Hill: University of North Carolina Press, 2018).

2. Ronald L. Lewis, "From Peasant to Proletarian: The Migration of Southern Blacks to the Central Appalachian Coalfields," *Journal of Southern History* 55, no. 1 (1989): 77–102.

Chapter 4

A Preliminary Taxonomy of the Blue Ridge Taco

Daniel S. Margolies

TACOS ARE the only food sold at the rodeo (called a *jaripeo*) held twice a month at La Gran Plaza México in Harmony, North Carolina. The tacos available there come in the popular varieties common at such Mexican events—*al pastor* (spicy marinated pork), *carnitas* (fried pork), *carne asada* (steak), *lengua* (tongue), *chorizo* (spicy sausage), *tripas* (intestines), and *pollo* (chicken), either stewed or fried. They are served, properly, with the choice of meat piled on two small tortillas of about four inches in diameter. These tacos are street taco style, small for ready consumption and in double stacked tortillas for structural integrity. The machine-made tortillas are heated in oil in astonishing numbers on a portable nickel grill top, placed and replaced on the heat by a worker exclusively focused on the task.

Cooks furiously and constantly cook meat. Handed off to the line servers, the tortillas and meat become tacos very quickly. There is, after all, a long line of people, and there are drinking and dancing to attend to. The pressing lines and exhaustingly loud music do not seem to disturb the servers, who prepare the tacos with evident care and respect for the food and the heavy-drinking clientele.

Carne asada, steaming and caramelized to crispy on the edges, is lifted from grease-filled chafing dishes and piled on the warm tortillas by plastic-gloved hands. Carnitas is served with generous additions of fat. Tripas is fried to an ideal crispiness so the tubes crackle when bitten. The lengua is boiled and very tender. Atop go chopped white onions and cilantro. The benediction is the corona of slivered radishes placed on top of everything on the plate.

Tacos are served at the top edge of the enormous dirt amphitheater. The taco stand seating area, which serves maybe fifty people at a time, is not empty until almost the end of the event. Most people I observe eat four to six tacos.

Though taco serving is localized at the jaripeo, beer is drunk everywhere. The only beer available is Modelo Especial in a can. People standing at the edge of the rodeo ring, watching the bull rides and listening to the bands playing nonstop, keep a bucket of beer and ice at their feet. Young men walk through the crowd hefting arresting amounts of Modelo. Dancing doesn't usually start until the bull riding is over. The early stages are for drinking and getting ready. Beer is sold by the bucket or by the case. It is, in fact, possible to ask for a single beer, but not many seem to bother. Servers sometimes seem a bit bemused at such a small order.

The atmosphere is festive and fun, sustaining a celebratory day-drinking vibe rather than the slightly menacing feel sometimes produced at heavy-drinking rodeo and music events in other places. The doors at the Gran Plaza México open at two in the afternoon on Sundays, and the music and partying of the jaripeo continues for more than ten relentless and exhilarating hours. The transnational cultures of food, drink, and music at the jaripeo are intertwined and inseparable.

The whole combined sensory and culinary experience at Gran Plaza México helps highlight the globalized changes in the contemporary Blue Ridge and in the Nuevo South more broadly. Even the location of Gran Plaza México signals a critical and ongoing cultural shift—or possibly a replenishing of an existing culture now stressed by socioeconomic changes. Gran Plaza México rests on sacred musical ground in Iredell County, which bills itself as "the Crossroads for the Future." Harmony is a storied southern place with a deep, evocative, and now faded history for bluegrass and old-time musicians. The VanHoy Farms Family Campground served as the longtime home of the Ole Time Fiddler's and Bluegrass Festival, which developed out of the Union Grove Fiddler's festival begun in 1924 in the community of Union Grove. That festival eventually spawned two competing festivals run by Van Hoy brothers: the World's Championship Old-Time Fiddlers Convention and the Ole Time Fiddler's and Bluegrass Festival. Iterations of these events with very similar names continued for some time and still occur today.[1] There is no existing evidence that tacos were served at any of them. Nowadays this once-iconic Van Hoy venue at the heart of southern musical culture has been born again as the heart of a new Mexican jaripeo tradition. La Gran Plaza México perfectly encapsulates Mexican placemaking in the Blue Ridge South, a process that has transformed the spaces, food, culture, and sounds of this corner of the Blue Ridge foothills.

Numerous scholars have explored the critical role of food in the ways immigrants reshape their new world (termed placemaking) and express their identities.[2] Mexican food historian Jeffrey M. Pilcher notes that "the study of food and the methodologies of food studies—including a careful attention to sensory perceptions and a critical perspective on constructions of authenticity—can contribute to our understanding of new social and cultural patterns that result from diverse migratory encounters."[3] Foodways play essential roles in helping produce what Setha Low calls "embodied space," which is "the location where human experience and consciousness take on material and spatial form."[4] In Appalachia, which is an embodied space if there ever was one, *where* you eat can matter as much as *what* you eat.

Appalachia is a region with a strong sense of place. As Barbara Ellen Smith and Stephen L. Fisher write, "Place is above all a collective product, experience, and possibility."[5] Food author Ronni Lundy quotes pastry chef Lisa Donovan as saying "I think there's a biological imperative that has us seeking a sense of place. . . . I'd wandered the whole planet wondering where my place was" until finding it in ancestral southwest Virginia.[6] The tacos at the jaripeo and elsewhere define a lot of what it means to eat situated in place in the globalized Appalachian South these days. Southern Appalachia is now recognized as a major nontraditional destination for contemporary Mexican migration, which has produced an attendant shift in sensory experience in the region.

Demographers designate the South as a region of "hypergrowth," and in southern Appalachia, the Latino population has doubled or even tripled in the recent past. The Latino percentage of the population of states such as Alabama, Georgia, and South Carolina is higher in the Appalachian areas than in non-Appalachian ones. Mexicans make up the majority of the migrants in most of these southern states. Approximately three-quarters of the migrant population in North Carolina is from Mexico, principally from the states of Guerrero, Veracruz, Guanajuato, Michoacán, Hidalgo, Oaxaca, Estado de México, and Puebla, and also from Mexico City. Migrants come to the region to work via many routes, both enticed by labor recruiters and drawn to newly established migrant and family networks and communities for jobs in agriculture, manufacturing, construction, landscaping, food service, and other fields that often become dominated by recent immigrants.[7] Employment diversification tends to expand over time, but as Sara Gleave and Qingfang Wang have established in comparative research on Knoxville and other southern cities, "while social capital and job information networks can positively impact a foreign-born individual's access to employment, they may also promote the concentration of these individuals in particular industries with a highly co-ethnic work force."[8] Migrant foodways, like all southern foodways, have emerged from the nexus of community, work, resource availability, and ingenuity. All of the changes have allowed tacos to become such an omnipresent aspect of southern foodways that it is almost easy to overlook them.

Tacos have inordinate symbolic heft for a seemingly simple food. The taco has its own literature and quite passionate partisans. Studying tacos functions as a shorthand to gain access to deeper and broader analyses of the U.S. interaction with Mexican migration and Mexican-American culture. Tacos have their own festivals across the country from Los Angeles to Detroit. "Who doesn't love Tacos?" asks the traveling Taco Festival, which hits cities as far-flung as Flagstaff, Cincinnati, Lafayette (Louisiana), Nashville, and Des Moines.[9]

Considering the taco for the first time in the Appalachian context is an excellent way to explore the region's evolving foodways and its cultural transformation. I am not presenting either a culinary or a cultural history of the taco, both of which have been covered in detail elsewhere.[10] The significance of the Blue Ridge tacos is not that they are especially different from those served in the borderlands of the Southwest and West or that they have blended with local foodways. Tacos are commonplace. What is interesting and important is that tacos are suddenly both ubiquitous and utilitarian in a region in which they once did not appear at all. They have become part of the foodways of today's Appalachia.

Tacos, *taquerias* (taco joints), taco trucks, and taco consumption are everywhere in the region nowadays. Where exactly are tacos made and what kind are they? I propose a taxonomy of Appalachian taco culture to serve as a guide to the taco-obsessed seeking the best food on offer in the rapidly changing region. My taxonomy also illustrates the range of tacos in the region and contextualizes both the new foodways and the taco's role in migrant placemaking. This taxonomy of the Blue Ridge taco provides a geography of the region's tacos and a consideration of their varied forms and realization.

If food is made with love of place as well as love of the ingredients and preparation, the love comes through. You can taste love in a well-made Blue Ridge taco just as you can in the functional artistry of other Appalachian food. In the best cases in many areas of contemporary Appalachia, you can find tacos made with love. These tacos might just be the foods that save America.

A PRELIMINARY TAXONOMY OF THE BLUE RIDGE TACO

My taxonomy of the Blue Ridge taco has a four-part classification. I could create even finer distinctions or other categories, but via a rigorous method of interviews, several thousand miles of taco hunting, and happy participant-observation through eating, I am confident that this four-part scheme accurately characterizes the contemporary taco landscape of the Blue Ridge.

1. THE ALL-TOO-COMMON TACO

The first category is also the easiest to describe and the easiest to dispatch. This category includes fast-food tacos and the many varieties of taco-like units served at Tex-Mex-style restaurants readily found throughout the entire region. These are not traditional, good, or creative tacos, but they do require classification because of their total saturation of even the tiniest hamlets of the southern Appalachians.

On a driving tour encompassing Appalachian Virginia, West Virginia, Tennessee, and North Carolina, I followed a careful methodology that was equal parts strategic scouting, local queries, and taco consumption. One ultimately useless but instructive way to find out about tacos in unfamiliar areas was to strike up conversations in public places and ask people where one could eat tacos. The answers tracked very closely to cultural origins. Asking local white Appalachians about their favorite taco place yielded essential uniform responses that became wearyingly similar: I was invariably directed to Taco Bell. This was done with sincerity and helpfulness. Many folks followed that up with the earnest and heartfelt explanation that they *really liked* to eat tacos.

It might be possible to write this chapter without deigning to discuss Taco Bell, and we can certainly sidestep consideration of the quality or meaning of the food served there. But it is worth considering for a moment the significance of the chain's ubiquity in Appalachia. Taco Bell has remarkable penetration in Appalachian markets. For example, there are five separate locations apiece in Roanoke, Knoxville, Johnson City, and Charleston, West Virginia; four in Asheville; and three in Bristol. Smaller Appalachian locales like Beckley, West Virginia; Harlan, Kentucky; or Grundy, Virginia, have at least one. That this form of "Mexican food" has become a standard item of fast-food diets is an interesting marker of cultural shift as significant, at least, as the transformation of pizza from Italian specialty to commonplace American fast food. Taco Bell ingredients are cooked elsewhere in a central facility and heated in plastic bags onsite.[11] Gustavo Arellano describes these tacos as "Mexican grub sold . . . fast, cheap, and with only a smattering of ethnicity."[12]

Taco Bell fast-food tacos have an even more common cousin in the tacos served at self-identified Mexican restaurants that can be found absolutely everywhere in the region. The common style of taco outside of the fast food setting takes a typical form. The tortilla is a commercially produced hard shell. Meats tend to be limited to minimally seasoned or unseasoned ground beef or chicken. These tacos are served with iceberg lettuce and some variant of what Kraft calls Mexican-style shredded cheddar jack cheese. Sometimes diced tomatoes are added on top. The ingredients are often prefabricated and the assemblage follows this aesthetic.

Tiny Saltville, Virginia, with a population of around two thousand people, has a Mexican restaurant called El Burrito Loco. The logo is a large mustachioed man wearing an enormous sombrero and a Mexican-style blanket and hoisting two maracas, all while riding a laughing burro. The caricature is more potent than the food. El Burrito Loco is part of a regional chain with branches in Glade Spring, Richlands, and Rural Retreat. Their tacos come in both hard shells or soft flour tortillas. The chicken is stewed, and served in the tortilla with iceberg lettuce and a red salsa thickened to the consistency of ketchup. Similar tacos can be found at restaurants in small towns and midsize cities across the region like the Hacienda Mexican Restaurants in West Virginia, Los Amigos in Gilbert, West Virginia, or the Azteca Mexican restaurant in Erwin, Tennessee. The food is indistinguishable in most respects from the generic food termed Mexican found throughout the United States. But it is significant that the Los Jalapeños Mexican Restaurant in Unicoi, Tennessee (a chain with another location in Piney Flats), sits next to a Walmart carved into the edge of the national forest along an interstate. What could be more common and more utilitarian in the Appalachian South today than a generic taco shop next to a Walmart?

2. THE TACO TRUCK TACO

During the presidential campaign of 2016, which was marked notably by racist, anti-Mexican pronouncements from Republican presidential candidate Donald Trump, Marco Gutierrez founded a group called Latinos for Trump. In a television interview, Gutierrez warned that "my culture is a very dominant culture, and it's imposing and it's causing problems. If you don't do something about it, you're going to have taco trucks on every corner." This comment provoked widespread expressions of appreciation for tacos as well as ridicule, including many from people enthusiastic at this prospect. One woman wrote on Twitter "#TacoTrucksOnEveryCorner sounds like the real American dream to me."[13] Even a conservative writer like Richard Cromwell celebrated the taco truck: "Whether you go with carnitas, lengua, chorizo, pollo, carne asada, cochinita, barbacoa, or some combination of all the aforementioned goodness, tacos are like manna from heaven. Making them more widely available has absolutely no downsides." The list of upsides he identified included "promoting free(er) avocado trade," economic mobility for workers, education, and even improved neighborhood watches. Cromwell concluded, "I mean really, why is this even a question?

We're talking about tacos here. Nutritious, delicious tacos. This is something we should all be able to agree on and which should unite us as Americans of all stripes. If you do not believe in tacos, and that they should be as widely available as possible, then there is only one obvious fact. You, sir, are a Communist, and we didn't build this great nation so grubby pinkos like you could destroy it."[14]

Tacos produced in taco trucks for immigrant communities can be considered something of an American classic, as these tacos were first realized on the West Coast in other, older migrant spaces.[15] Taco truck tacos came into existence with a specific functionality, defined structure, and built-in audience for consumption. Taco truck tacos in the Blue Ridge might be considered the ones with the greatest Mexican or West Coast influence in terms of origins, but the tacos they serve are provided by, and are made for, a transnational population of workers embedded in the region.

There are taco trucks to be found all over the Blue Ridge, tucked on the side of the road, pulled up to large job sites, or parked next to one of the even more common *tiendas* (Mexican stores). The trucks appear in what can be thought of as "loose spaces" of newly globalizing areas. A fascinating set of reshaped migrant spaces in Appalachia are the "loose spaces" of the region, or what Karen A. Franck and Quentin Stevens call the "left over spaces and abandoned spaces." These loose spaces are unorganized, unused, and ripe for reimagination by migrants creating new home places. These spaces include the "nothing" spaces of globalization and modern America such as roadsides, abandoned downtowns, decaying strip malls, and now-emptied community or church buildings. Franck and Stevens argue that "for a site to become loose, people themselves must recognize the possibilities inherent in it and make use of those possibilities for their own ends, facing the potential risks of doing so." Such spaces, they argue persuasively, are excellent for "nurtur[ing] particularity in the urban public realm, sustaining local practices and allowing the identity of place and culture to flourish."[16] Such loose spaces riddle Appalachia, which has endured wrenching economic change over time.

In the loose spaces I visited in Appalachia, the taco trucks and
taco trailers freshly reorganize spaces additionally functioning
as nodes of community interaction as much as sites of consumption. Taco trucks parked on the edge of a road or in the corner of
a parking lot suddenly anchor vibrant points of social interaction.
They fill an interstitial food and social space. In Swannanoa, North
Carolina, the Tacos Jalisco taco trailer pulled by a pickup provides
opportunities for men (I have only seen men there, as at many
taco trucks in the region) to hang out in an otherwise unnoticeable
space on the side of the road in front of a small house. A line of stools
gives people a place to sit. In rural Surry County, North Carolina,
another taco trailer built out of an RV parked transversely in front
of a house allows the driveway to be reshaped into a public meeting space, complete with wooden stools. Dos Padres taco truck in
Asheville parks in front of the Carpet Connection in a strip mall.
This truck relocated from San Miguel, California. The owner left an
area of intense competition and high expense for one with strong
potential for profit.

In Mount Airy, North Carolina, the Los Amigos taco trailer sits
next to La Tapatia 3 tienda and serves food prepared and served
with evident skill and love. Unlike fast-food tacos prepared from
prefabricated ingredients, these tacos take time to prepare. There
are a lot of choices of meat available, each of which is stencil spray-
painted on the side of the trailer. The choices include expected
varieties like carne asada and al pastor, as well as less common ones
like *barbacoa, suadero, cabeza,* and *cecina* that are only available in
places catering specifically to migrant populations. None of these
fillings is at all rare for tacos; they are the standards. But they are
not very common in the Blue Ridge, and they are produced for a
specialty migrant customer base. It is also striking that this and
other taco trucks offer, rapidly and for only a few dollars, such a
wide array of foods requiring time-consuming, difficult, and skillful
preparation. This is real food, slow cooked and hand prepared, but
designed to be sold cheaply and eaten quickly. Taco truck tacos are
rapidly prepared but liberated from the real problems associated

with the industrial food system destroying American health. The cuts of meats are different as well, presenting food sourcing that pushes beyond the Sysco-supplied kitchens that dominate other foodways in America to a stunning extent.[17]

Consider the types of meats available from Los Amigos in tacos, tortas, burritos, or other forms. Suadero is a common street taco filling made of a unique mixture of meats from the underside of cows, soft in texture but uniquely and time-consumingly fried to be crispy. Cecina is laboriously prepared by salting and marinating meat before cooking. Slowly cooked barbacoa is a flavorful and extremely tender meat of the cheek and other parts of the head, usually of cows but not uncommonly of goats. Cabeza, as the name suggests, comes from the head. Los Amigos used what tasted like cheek-heavy beef for the barbacoa. Both were delicious. The tortillas at Los Amigos are not handmade, but they are produced locally in North Carolina. Carne asada and al pastor tacos are served with white onions and cilantro, radishes, and several kinds of home-made salsa.

A hallmark of taco truck tacos in the Blue Ridge is their affordability. This is in keeping with the functional role of food truck food. Some of this functionality allows for the expansion of the range of the taco trucks into hybridized versions. For example, the Taqueria El Paso taco truck in Christiansburg, Virginia, appears aimed at an audience midway between the working-class migrant constituency of traditional taco trucks and the wider general population. It is parked on the road across from the Corning, Inc., plant and in front of a strip mall with a tienda, a workout studio, and other small businesses. Down the road are typical strip mall chain stores. At lunchtime, Taqueria El Paso is very busy. There is a line of people, many clearly working-class men wearing clothes covered in drywall dust, construction workers, and cops. Others are evidently college students from nearby universities, or office workers. The truck has tripas and lengua, though they are more expensive than other varieties. I was asked if I wanted cheese on my tacos, which I observed was not a question asked of everybody (that is, not asked of people who looked Latino). I took the question to be practical in intent rather than transgressive. This was a taco truck that understood its function in a diverse area of dynamic growth and change.

The advent of the taco truck in the Blue Ridge gives a glimpse of much of what a taco offers as a distinct street food—accessibility, low cost, efficient and energy-intensive nutrition, and of course variety and deliciousness. In my subjective and anecdotal experience, it is much rarer to have mediocre food at a taco truck than at a place serving the common tacos. Taco truck tacos are no more "real" than those common tacos. However, as Jeff Rice has observed in writing about craft beer, "craft can be the space where objects interact with humans and other objects to produce a network of relationships."[18] What I have discovered is that taco trucks—and their tacos—promise a moment of spatial respite along with the opportunity to eat real and purposeful food that is largely missing in the common tacos. Simple, yet finely honed and meaningful, these taco truck tacos in many ways seem like the ideal food for a region that shares the same characteristics.

3. THE TAQUERIA TACO

Taquerias, restaurants focusing on quick preparation of tacos where one generally orders at a counter and tacos are made to order, are an absolutely standard institution in other regions, particularly in the borderlands of the Southwest and West. They not uncommonly engender a fierce loyalty among taco aficionados.[19] Taquerias are a fairly new addition to the Blue Ridge that in many ways are a more profound marker of regional and culinary transformation than even the expressive and significant arrival of taco trucks. These tacos are purposeful, often very similar to the style and range of tacos available in the trucks. The tortillas are sometimes handmade and sometimes machine made. Generally, there is a wide range of fillings offered, and the menus include other items like quesadillas and burritos. The tacos are sometimes state-of-the-art hybrid tacos made with uncommon ingredients meant to appeal to broader audiences. But the innovative edge of hybrid taqueria tacos in the Blue Ridge remains connected to their utilitarian background as a working-class food. Taquerias are locales for functional food.

Each of these taqueria spaces provides a market-oriented and highly stylized recapitulation of Mexican imagery, music, and foodways in the regional sensory landscape. A tienda y taqueria fills loose space and serves as a de facto community center as well as a place to eat. Migrants seeking an economic and cultural footing in their new environment may be uniquely drawn to these loose spaces.[20] For example, El Mexicana Tienda Latina in rural Fairview Crossroads, North Carolina, does more than sell food and clothing; it provides space for a dozen young men to watch Mexican boxing on a rainy Sunday afternoon. The Taqueria Fast in Weaverville, North Carolina, has the appearance of a restaurant but actually uses a taco truck parked behind the building as its kitchen. Waitresses take orders, then walk out of the building and place the order at the taco truck. It is not easy to figure how this passes muster with restaurant inspectors, but the tacos are good and are served appropriately on doubled tortillas.

A taqueria typical of the region is the Tienda y Taqueria El Rosario in Collinsville, Virginia, which serves very traditional-style tacos at a small eating area. Painted to look like the Mexican flag, it stands colorfully and stridently next to a typical local institution in its own right, Southern Gun, Inc. These kinds of critical visual clues painted on taquerias, along with new foodways, can act as a solvent on regional distinctiveness in some cases and as an accelerant in others.[21]

Nowadays, taquerias are found throughout the southern Appalachians, though they are not as ubiquitous as the common Tex-Mex-style restaurants discussed earlier. It is not hard to come across them in towns like Maryville, Tennessee, or Ferrum, Virginia, or in cities like Asheville, Roanoke, Harrisonburg (Virginia), or Charleston (West Virginia). Transnationalism in foodways creates new experiences with cultural, economic, political, gender, and even spiritual dimensions, and the impact on individuals and institutions resonates in new ways within regional cultures.[22] La Mexicana Tienda y Taqueria, one of the older businesses surveyed, has been in Rocky Mount, Virginia, for more than ten years. It serves tacos of all the typical varieties on homemade tortillas, as well as tamales and other foods. It also meets the needs of a transnational population with specialty foods from fresh aloe leaves to hot sauces, numerous Catholic religious items, and essential financial services like transnational cash transfers.

Most of the migrant-oriented "true" taquerias in the region are connected to tiendas. In West Asheville, Taqueria Gonzalez moved locations and became Taqueria Muñoz, which is now connected to a full-service tienda. In contrast, Zia Taqueria Asheville not far away is directed to a nonmigrant clientele and clearly is using the term "taqueria" mainly as a signifier. It operates as a bar-restaurant with hybridized southwestern-style food and a generalized Anglo hipster sensibility.

4. THE HIPSTER TACO

Appalachian regional distinctiveness is dented like virtually everywhere else in the globalized capitalist realm today by a global hipster aesthetic reproducing itself locally with astonishing speed. You can recognize the signs in the old-timey lightbulbs, reclaimed wood, large beards, letterpress signs, craft beers, locally roasted coffee, and on and on.[23] Blue Ridge hipster tacos reflect the global hipster aesthetic encompassing the interconnections and complications of craft, commodity fetishism, and consumerism. Tacos produced in the global hipster mode are elements of style and identity formation, postmodern syncretism, and a particularly pungent form of consumerist capitalism as much as they are food. Ethnicity has an uncertain and fungible role in the hipster realm.[24] The taco is appropriated alongside the repurposing of other working-class markers like mill buildings, train depots, and other loose spaces now refitted for gentrifying areas in college towns and hipster meccas like Asheville. And, not unimportantly, along with hipster style come hipster prices. Rather than a working-class food designed for utilitarian efficiency and priced appropriately, hipster tacos are designed for a consumer class. They are pricier than other tacos, reflecting the expensively remodeled locales, novel ingredients, and higher costs of cities and college towns. Sometimes they are just plain overpriced.

Hipster tacos do not originate in the region, of course. They are regional manifestations of a national trend toward syncretic food. Much of the style comes, as such things often do, from California, where the Mexican-Korean fusion movement and bulgogi tacos began.[25] The hipster taco can be readily found nowadays in Johnson City, where there are at least three places within two blocks downtown that sell some variety of hipster tacos. One, the Korean Taco House, is actually a Korean place and so falls more into a fusionist category than a hipster one. A second, Holy Taco, around the corner, unquestionably caters to a hipster sensibility. Fillings available for tacos there include carne asada, carnitas, and pollo, as well as vegan "Thai Portobello," and lime- and jalapeño-seasoned tofu.

The third, the White Duck Taco Shop, is a chain with three locations in Asheville and elsewhere in the Southeast that best captures the hipster taco vibe. In Johnson City, White Duck is incorporated within the Yee-Haw Brewery taproom inside the Tweetsie Railroad Depot, a setting which presents something of a hipster trifecta. Interestingly, the White Duck Taco Shop makes no claims of authenticity. The menu is proud to claim that "we are committed to buying 99% American Made products," which might undermine the stance of a business trying to tie its bona fides to ethnic origins.

The tacos offered at White Duck are almost aggressively nontraditional, including "Banh Mi Tofu, Black Bean, Jerk Chicken, Crispy Chicken BLT, Spicy Buffalo Chicken, Bangkok Shrimp®, Lump Crab, Korean Beef Bulgogi, Steak & Cheese, Fish, Duck w/ Mole, Mushroom Potato w/ Romesco, Lamb Gyro, [and] Thai Peanut Chicken." The "Bangkok Shrimp®" is indeed trademarked in the menu. Tacos can be ordered with a side of kimchi or gazpacho.

My discussion of hipster tacos in the Blue Ridge might be taken as a fairly caustic reading, but it is not the only interpretation available. These tacos are often quite delicious to eat despite being nontraditional in presentation. They boast fresh ingredients, lavish and thoughtful spicing, and general attentiveness to the experiential aspects of food consumption. The "Bangkok Shrimp®" tacos were, for example, quite tasty despite the irritation factor of the ®. As virtually every taco writer points out, once upon a time even hypertraditional tacos al pastor were syncretic and transnational entities created by Lebanese immigrants to Mexico.[26]

Additionally, it seems important to observe that in self-aware hipster locales, one of the most common foods is a variant of the taco. This is clearly now a food for sustenance as well as a marker of good taste for a growing transnational elite in the region. Tacos have become more than an accoutrement of good taste. They have become crucial to contemporary millennial cultural traditions outside of the ethnic frame of their origins. Tacos have been both appropriated and incorporated.

This chapter is but a first step to a comprehensive geography of the taco in Appalachia. A full accounting of all these types of tacos may well be impossible largely because of the inherent mobilities of people and things in the region today. Taco trucks move, of course, and so too do numerous other migrant-owned businesses and migrant-frequented locales. They disappear over time, sometimes within surprising speed, or are replaced. Returning over months and years throughout the region, one of the few consistently unchanging spaces I have found has been the jaripeo at Gran Plaza México, where foodways and soundways signal a critical aspect of the emerging new cultural geography of the Blue Ridge. Taken together, all these examples demonstrate diverse and well-developed migrant food cultures reflecting and influencing a broad range of novel styles, interests, and uses. They clearly situate the Appalachian South as a newly vital new globalized borderland into which Mexican foodways properly must be folded. Most critically, these examples demonstrate the evolving and transnational sensibilities of migrant culinary expression in Appalachia and its adoption by diverse residents. My preliminary taxonomy presented here invites further exploration of the expansive connectivities and creativities of the Mexican diaspora in Appalachia.

NOTES

My thanks to Lora Smith, Elizabeth Engelhardt, Erica Abrams Locklear, the enthusiastic participants in the joint Grow Appalachia and Appalachian Food Summit at Berea College in 2016, and to the anonymous reviewers for their excellent comments.

1. "Crossroad for the Future" is on a sign at the Iredell County line observed by the author, 2016. An event continues at The Van Hoy Farms Family Campground, which lists itself in Union Grove. Gran Plaza México, which occurs at the exact same place, uses Harmony as its location. Nobody could give a clear answer why this was the case. See http://vanhoyfarms.com/fiddlers-convention/.

2. Arijit Sen, "Food, Place, and Memory: Bangladeshi Fish Stores on Devon Avenue, Chicago," *Food and Foodways* 24, nos. 1–2 (January–June 2016): 67–88; Ian Cook and Philip Crang, "The World on a Plate: Culinary Culture, Displacement and Geographical Knowledges," *Journal of Material Culture* 1, no. 2 (1996): 131–53. On immigrant placemaking in the South, see Jamie Winders, "Re-Placing Southern Geographies: The Role of Latino Migration in Transforming the South, Its Identities, and Its Study," *Southeastern Geographer* 51, no. 2 (Summer 2011): 342–58; Holly R. Barcus, "The Emergence of New Hispanic Settlement Patterns in Appalachia," *Professional Geographer* 59, no. 3 (2007): 298–315; Heather A. Smith and Owen J. Furuseth, eds., *Latinos in the New South: Transformations of Place* (Burlington, VT: Ashgate, 2007); Helen B. Marrow, *New Destination Dreaming: Immigration, Race, and Legal Status in the Rural American South* (Stanford, CA: Stanford University Press, 2011); Jamie Winders, "Bringing Back the (B)order: Post-9/11 Politics of Immigration, Borders, and Belonging in the Contemporary U.S. South," *Antipode* 39, no. 5 (2007): 921–23; Barbara Ellen Smith and Jamie Winders, "'We're Here to Stay': Economic Restructuring, Latino Migration and Place-Making in the U.S. South," *Transactions of the Institute of British Geographers* 33, no. 1 (January 2008): 60–72; Kelly Main and Gerardo Francisco Sandoval, "Placemaking in a Translocal Receiving

Community: The Relevance of Place to Identity and Agency," *Urban Studies* 52, no. 1 (January 2015): 71–86.

3. Jeffrey M. Pilcher, "'Old Stock' Tamales and Migrant Tacos: Taste, Authenticity, and the Naturalization of Mexican Food," *Social Research* 81, no. 2 (Summer 2014): 443.

4. Setha Low, "Placemaking and Embodied Space," in *Making Place: Space and Embodiment in the City,* ed. Arijit Sen and Lisa Silverman (Bloomington: Indiana University Press, 2014), 19.

5. Barbara Ellen Smith and Stephen L. Fisher, *Transforming Places: Lessons from Appalachia* (Champaign: University of Illinois Press, 2012), 267. Discussing the intertwinings of social power and political economy of place in Appalachia, Smith and Fisher write, "This means that, in specific places across Appalachia, the effects of wider social processes are becoming more transparent and palpable, and the interconnections among diverse places, political issues, and social groups are becoming more dense" (282).

6. Donovan is quoted in Ronni Lundy, *Victuals: An Appalachian Journey, with Recipes* (New York: Clarkson Potter, 2016), 86.

7. On migration to Appalachia, see Rakesh Kochhar, Roberto Suro, and Sonya Tafoya, "The New Latino South: The Context and Consequences of Rapid Population Growth," Pew Hispanic Center, July 26, 2005, http://pewhispanic.org/reports/report.php?ReportID=50; Barcus, "Emergence of New Hispanic Settlement Patterns," 298–304; Kelvin Pollard and Linda A. Jacobsen, "The Appalachian Region in 2010: A Census Data Overview, Prepared for the Appalachian Regional Commission," September 2011, https://assets.prb.org/pdf12/appalachia-census-chartbook-2011.pdf, 19.

8. Sara Gleave and Qingfang Wang, "Foreign-Born Latino Labor Market Concentration in Six Metropolitan Areas in the U.S. South," *Southeastern Geographer* 53, no. 2 (2013): 160. For a study of rural economic and work activity in North Carolina that also pays attention to spatiality and placemaking, see Owen J. Furuseth, "A New Rural North Carolina: Latino Place-Making and Community Engagement," in *The Next Rural Economies: Constructing Rural Place in Global Economies,* ed. Greg Halseth, Sean Patrick Markey, and David Bruce (Cambridge: CAB International, 2010), 45–57.

9. https://thetacofestival.com/, accessed September 2016.

10. Jeffrey M. Pilcher, *Planet Taco: A Global History of Mexican Food* (Oxford: Oxford University Press, 2012); Déborah Holtz and Juan Carlos Mena, *Tacopedia* (London: Phaidon, 2015); Gustavo Arellano,

Taco USA: How Mexican Food Conquered America (New York: Scribner, 2013). Important work on tacos in the South is being done under the guidance of Steven Alvarez's taco literacy project at the University of Kentucky. This effort has achieved that rare combination of finely wrought academic theorization, pedagogical usefulness, and popular media fascination. See Gustavo Arellano, "Are You Taco Literate? Lessons from Steven Alvarez," *Gravy* 62 (Winter 2016), http://www.southernfoodways.org/are-you-taco-literate/. See also "Welcome," https://tacoliteracy.com/2016/01/08/welcome/.

11. There is a useful app called the Taco Bell Locator, https://www.tacobell.com/locations. On the transformation of other formerly ethnic foods into American fast food, see Hasia Diner, *Hungering for America: Italian, Irish and Jewish Foodways in the Age of Migration* (Cambridge, MA: Harvard University Press, 2001); Carol Helstosky, *Pizza: A Global History* (London: Reaktion Books, 2008); Michael P. Mariano and Margaret S. Crocco, "Pizza: Teaching US History through Food and Place," *Social Studies* 106, no. 4 (July–August 2015): 149–58. See also Petula Dvorak, "Taco Trucks: As American as Lo Mein and Pizza Pie," *Washington Post*, September 5, 2016. On Taco Bell cooking techniques, see Pilcher, *Planet Taco*, 3.

12. Arellano, *Taco USA*, 64.

13. Chokshi, Niraj, "'Taco Trucks on Every Corner': Trump Supporter's Anti-Immigration Warning," *New York Times*, September 2, 2016.

14. Richard Cromwell, "7 Reasons America Needs a Taco Truck on Every Corner," *The Federalist*, September 2, 2016, http://thefederalist.com/2016/09/02/7-reasons-america-needs-taco-truck-every-corner/.

15. A nice survey is Lynn Brown, "The Rise of the Taco Truck," *JSTOR Daily*, March 6, 2017, https://daily.jstor.org/rise-of-the-taco-truck/, which also relies heavily on Jeffrey M. Pilcher, "Was the Taco Invented in Southern California?" *Gastronomica* 8, no. 1 (Winter 2008): 26–38.

16. Karen A. Franck and Quentin Stevens, "Tying Down Loose Space," in *Loose Space: Possibility and Diversity in Urban Life*, ed. Karen A. Franck and Quentin Stevens (London: Routledge, 2007), 8, 20–21. I have applied this concept of loose spaces to Appalachian visual culture in "*Taquerias* and *Tiendas* in the Blue Ridge: Viewing the Transformation of Space in a Globalized Appalachia," *Appalachian Journal* 39, nos. 3–4 (Spring–Summer 2012): 246–68.

17. Ulrich Boser, "Every Bite You Take: How Sysco Came to Monopolize Most of What You Eat," *Slate*, February 21, 2007, http://www.slate.com/articles/life/food/2007/02/every_bite_you_take.html.

18. For a rhetorical analysis of contemporary craft brewing, and the larger deployments of ideas of craft versus technology in food, see Jeff Rice, *Craft Obsession: The Social Rhetorics of Beer* (Carbondale: Southern Illinois University Press, 2016), x–xiii.

19. For an example, see David Plotnikoff, "Ciudad de los Tacos: The Complete Guide to All the Taquerias of Redwood City, v. 2.0," http://www.emeraldlake.com/tacos/.

20. Marie Price and Courtney Whitworth argue that "it is the betweenness-of-place demanded by the transnational realities of immigrant life that begs for a different understanding of space." Marie Price and Courtney Whitworth, "Soccer and Latino Cultural Space: Metropolitan Washington *Fútbol* Leagues," in *Hispanic Spaces, Latino Places: Community and Cultural Diversity in Contemporary America,* ed. Daniel D. Arreola (Austin: University of Texas Press, 2004), 169.

21. Arjun Appadurai, "Disjuncture and Difference in the Global Cultural Economy," in *Modernity at Large: Cultural Dimensions of Globalization* (Minneapolis: University of Minnesota Press, 1996), 27–43.

22. Daniel Mato, "On the Making of Transnational Identities in the Age of Globalization: The U.S. Latina/o-'Latin' American Case," *Cultural Studies* 12, no. 4 (October 1998): 598–620; Bryan R. Roberts, Reanne Frank, and Fernando Lozano-Ascencio, "Transnational Migrant Communities and Mexican Migration to the US," *Ethnic and Racial Studies* 22, no. 2 (March 1999): 238–66.

23. Kyle Chayka, "Same Old, Same Old: How the Hipster Aesthetic Is Taking Over the World," *Guardian,* August 6, 2016, https://www.theguardian.com/commentisfree/2016/aug/06/hipster-aesthetic-taking-over-world; see also Sharon Zukin, "Reconstructing the Authenticity of Place," *Theory and Society* 40, no. 2 (March 2011): 161–65.

24. Adam J. Mathews, "Exploring Place Marketing by American Microbreweries: Neolocal Expressions of Ethnicity and Race," *Journal of Cultural Geography* 33, no. 3 (2016): 275.

25. David Brindley, "How One Korean Taco Truck Launched an $800 Million Industry," *National Geographic Magazine,* July 2015, http://ngm.nationalgeographic.com/2015/07/food-trucks/brindley-text.

26. Pilcher, *Planet Taco,* 267; Sarah Portnoy, *Food, Health, and Culture in Latino Los Angeles* (Lanham, MD: Rowan and Littlefield, 2017), 76.

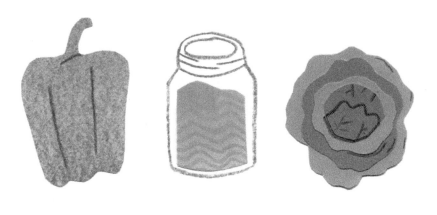

Poem

Chowchow

Jeff Mann

Save for the spices—celery seed,
mustard seed, cinnamon and cloves—

my father's grown it all: cabbage
plump enough to fill a lap,

green bell peppers' shredded jade,
the red cayenne and Hungarian hot

arching inside like cathedral naves
carved from ruby, intense to eye and tongue,

Jeff Mann

the High Romantics of the garden.
Come morning-glory season

he puts it up, that regional oddity from
a better America, before McDonald's

and strip malls swallowed the cornfields.
Chowchow tastes like childhood,

like ancestry, and so we cherish it,
summers stalled behind Ball jar glass.

Our future's a bowl of beans—
cranberry, pinto, yellow eye—

simmered with bacon grease,
steaming the winter windows,

served with hot cornbread, black sorghum,
a jar of chowchow brought up from the basement.

Chapter 5

An Education in Beans

Abigail Huggins

DURING MY childhood in North Carolina, my family casually enjoyed beans in the summer. I have memories of stringing fresh green beans on the porch and expecting butter beans as a staple on Grandma's stove when we showed up for dinner. More often than not, though, beans were from a can from the grocery store—a tolerable vegetable in the world of quick meals in which we were raised, where our working parents did the best they knew to do. Beans were in our repertoire, but they were not necessarily foundational, understood, or beloved.

In the summer of 2016, I found myself getting schooled in beans—their specificity, their diversity, their meaning, their adoration. Mostly, I was learning that bean knowledge is vast and endless. I was in eastern Kentucky, studying community foodways through oral history as a graduate student in Southern studies.[1] Through a series of connections, I landed in Letcher County, where intersections among community initiatives were connecting food access and farmer support.[2] Valerie Horn, of Community Farm Alliance, graciously introduced me to people who introduced me to more people. With food as a starting point—but not necessarily an ending point—I found myself interviewing farmers, gardeners, seed savers, foragers, and activists. I listened to the stories people chose to share about their lives and communities. For many, food was central to their memories, passions, and hopes. And while people discussed a variety of foods—sauerkraut, gingerbread, tomato juice, and wild edibles—each worthy of their own reflection, beans stood out as a significant food in Kentuckians' lives. Beans connected stories of seed saving, community gatherings, and food preservation to calls for attention to place, mindfulness of earlier generations, and forethought for generations to come. In the interviews, beans not only sustained bodies, they also functioned as metaphors for ways of being.

When I interviewed Brandon Jent, a young activist and scholar who was working as a VISTA member with the Cowan Community Center, he said something that will always stick with me: "I want something that was important to people before me to be important to people after me, through me."[3] Brandon was specifically talking about a history of singing in his family as a tradition he intends to pass on. His insight crystallized for me a larger theme of generational awareness that I heard among other interviewees. It inspired the title of my thesis: "Before Me, After Me, Through Me: Stories of Food and Community in Eastern Kentucky."[4] In a thread woven through conversations, people expressed a mindfulness of families and communities of the past in tandem with a responsibility to create livable communities for future generations. Over and over, I witnessed culture that is both rooted and dynamic, both traditional and evolutionary, both story-driven and innovative. This brings me back to beans. The act of saving bean seeds is a way of bringing the past into the future through careful work in the present. Bean varieties matter: for taste, fullness, color, family history, and connection to place. Each seed saver has a reason they've passed on particular beans over generations. Beans tell a deep history in these mountains, the first beans having been grown by indigenous people long before white people arrived.[5]

A few narrators in this project recognized the history of indigenous peoples in their discussions of foodways and beans, even if they did not have direct connections themselves. The interviewees here vary in age, class, and gender, but they are not diverse in race or ethnicity. With more time and relationship building, I hope to conduct a wider collection of oral histories, better representative of the racial diversity of the region, including indigenous, immigrant, and African American populations. A constant is likely to remain: deep respect for beans' role in connecting and sustaining communities.

Several people told me stories about family and community bean seeds. As I rocked on a swing in Glenn Brown's front yard in Whitesburg, in eyesight of his early summer garden, he shared his methods of saving seeds, including particular bean seeds he's been growing out for eighty years, since he was a child, that his father saved before him:

All my seed beans, I pick the best ones out before I gather them. I leave them on the vine, all my best beans. Sometimes I even leave a little section of it. Well, they turn yellow. Now that they get good and yellow, I pick them and lay them on the picnic table. Let them dry, like shucky beans. Then I hull them out and separate them. But, I've started putting them in the freezer now. Most of them, I put some in the jars because, I have so many, I can't get them all in the freezer. But, most of the time, they keep four or five years. Every year, I take some out that I've got over four- or five-year-old. I forget how many I got, I guess about thirty-five [varieties] now. I got two off of Bill Best, up here, Saturday, greasy, some kind of a greasy grit. I've heard of them, but I've never seen them. They don't even look like green beans, but that's what they are. And I got promised two or three other kinds. Supposed to be good beans. I don't like these old Blue Lakes or something like that. They raise them, pick them with a machine, and no telling what's in them, besides they're not very good to eat much. If you eat a good bean then eat a Blue Lake, you say, "What's wrong with that bean?" Not just Blue Lake, they're all about that way. One's I've got, my mainstay, I know they're good beans. So I save the seeds of all them. And I've had at least five of them for eighty year myself. I don't know how long Dad had them before that.[6]

Debbie Adams, a grower who sells at the Letcher County/City of Whitesburg Farmers' Market, was also excited to share tales of bean seeds. Growing old bean seed is what turned Debbie and her partner Woody into market gardeners when they had surplus vegetables. I'd heard versions of Debbie's bean story before, but as we sat down under a shade tree in her yard, just before summer showers set in, this is what she recounted:

My family always grew a garden, Woody's family always grew a garden, but, being young, that wasn't the route I wanted to go. And so, we never really grew a large garden or anything like that. Every once in a while, I'd grow cucumbers and tomatoes or a lettuce bed. And I had canned tomato juice and tomatoes and stuff like that, but never canning or doing anything on a big scale. So, when Woody got laid off in 2013, the following spring, my brother—we've always let him use our property to raise a garden—he was telling us, "Y'all might as well raise a garden, Woody ain't working now, Woody ain't working, y'all might as well raise a garden." So Woody and he got together and decided to raise us a small garden. Plant some potatoes and different things to have over the winter. And Woody came over one day from the garden and said, "You got any bean seeds?" And I said, "Oh my gosh, if I've got any, they're old." But, I keep all my seeds in the freezer. And I went out there and grabbed a bag of bean seeds, it said "1994" on them and I chuckled when I handed them to him. I said, "These things are twenty-year-old. There's no way they're going to grow." And, that year, we had six bushels of beans come off those twenty-year-old seeds. And, I was pleased.[7]

For Colette Quillen, who also sells at the Letcher County/City of Whitesburg Farmers' Market, bean seeds were a special family treasure that she sought out. As I interviewed Colette and her partner Bennett at their home in Deane, she talked about how she acquired a particular variety of white fall beans from her mother and how she intends to pass them on:

My mom, she would try to grow the white fall beans that was handed down from the family. They were very good. It was like she had something that nobody else had. She was tight and stingy with them, and she would not share them. So, after we got married, she wouldn't give me the seed. So somehow I bought some beans off of her. I bought them from her, which is strange. But, that's how I got the seed to them. So, what I'm trying to do is, I'm trying to give everybody seed to them, because they're very good and I don't want them to be lost. And there's nowhere else in the area that has those specific white fall beans. And they're high in demand. If anybody knows you've got them, they're like, "Yeah, I want those, you better make sure you save me some and I get them." And everybody you know is just like, they'll call you later, "I want those," they're that good.[8]

Don Maggard, a retired coal miner who is a market farmer and forager in Vicco, showed me around the bottom land where generations of his family have gardened. Next to a singing creek, looking out over his orderly bean trellises and other vegetables, he spoke of the importance of heirloom varieties of seeds and the way he cares for his family and community through gardening:

> I have goose beans, I have turkey creek tomatoes, I have turkey craw beans, and I have Venson-Watts tomatoes, and I have okra and about all of my beans are heirloom seeds, about all of them are heirloom. They're the old seed that we have, that I have accumulated over the last, say, ten or fifteen years myself. That I collected old seed from different people that have grown them for years. I have found out that using the heirloom seed that you have better production and they're bigger, more yield and they're just better for me to grow. And I grow sweet potatoes and I grow carrots, cabbage, and I don't know, just about anything that you can grow, I grow it. Mustard greens, lettuce, I grow all of that. And my, all of my brothers and sisters they usually eat from it and I eat from it and I just share it with the community around. Anybody that wants to can stop by and pick them a mess of beans if they want to or get them some cucumbers or whatever . . . My favorite is probably the greasy bean, the brown greasy bean. I like a color bean—and the red eye fall bean is probably one of my favorites too.[9]

Glenn Brown also told stories of the way beans brought a community together when he was growing up:

> Well, we'd have what they call a bean stringing, if you've ever heard of that. They'd make shucky beans, leather britches. . . . They'd go up to the house, their house, have four or five neighbors. Some of them would be stringing those beans, cleaning them. Another would have a needle and thread with a string on it. They'd just stick that needle through, and put them on, have them on big strings, shucky beans. Now, they put them in freezers, break them up and put them in freezers, mostly now. Sometimes we'd

have a little something to eat or even bigger ones they'd have a party, have somebody singing the banjo or guitar or something. So, it just seemed more like friends, it did, instead of neighbors.[10]

Gwen and Mable Johnson, a daughter and mother I interviewed at the Hemphill Community Center, shared memories of canning beans, laughing about the work they used to do compared to using a pressure canner now:

Mable: Green beans, everything. Corn. Now we didn't have a freezer then. And, we would can corn and beans outside in a washtub. What you do is fill the jars, put them in a big three-bushel tub, pad rags or paper boxes around them. Build you a fire under it. Her papaw on her daddy's side would cook from daylight to dark.

Gwen: I used to help carry the water and help stoke the fire under the tubs.

Mable: And they'd say, if it rains now, we got to put a piece of tin on top of them or all the jars would bust.

Gwen: It's the cold water as versus the hot water, the temperature change would break the jars. And the padding between them is because when they start cooking, they jiggle around and hit against each other, and they'll bust that way.

Mable: Now, we put them in a pressure canner, cook them 25 minutes.[11]

The technologies that many people referred to—such as freezers and pressure canners—allow for easier seed saving and food preservation.[12] Practices evolve over generations while people continue to pass on common values. The tastes of particular varieties of beans still matter. The importance of putting up summer's abundance for winter remains. The sharing of food and music in community persists. The kindness of growing extra to share with neighbors lives on. The past matters, but it is not all. The present and the future matter, but they are not all. The people I've gotten to know in eastern Kentucky taught me that traditions and stories matter, but they cannot remain stagnant. They must be grown out by each subsequent generation, carefully selected and passed on to the next.

NOTES

1. Oral history has a long presence in Appalachian studies scholarship. For more oral history scholarship on the region, see Alessandro Portelli, *They Say in Harlan County: An Oral History* (New York: Oxford University Press, 2010); Shannon Elizabeth Bell, *Our Roots Run Deep as Ironweed: Appalachian Women and the Fight for Environmental Justice* (Champaign: University of Illinois Press, 2013); Silas House and Jason Howard, *Something's Rising: Appalachians Fighting Mountaintop Removal* (Lexington: University Press of Kentucky, 2009).

2. Kassidy Stricklett, "Farmacy Program Promotes Healthier Lifestyle," *WYMT*, August 10, 2016, http://www.wymt.com/content/news/Farmacy-program-promotes-healthier-lifestyle-389805932.html.

3. Brandon Jent, interview by Abigail Huggins, July 18, 2016.

4. Abigail Huggins, "Before Me, After Me, Through Me: Stories of Food and Community in Eastern Kentucky," master's thesis, University of Mississippi, 2017; Abigail Huggins, "Eastern Kentucky Food Stories," https://ekyfoodstories.wordpress.com/.

5. For more Appalachian bean history, see Bill Best, *Saving Seeds, Preserving Taste: Seed Savers in Appalachia* (Athens: Ohio University Press, 2013); Ronni Lundy, *Victuals: An Appalachian Journey, with Recipes* (New York: Clarkson Potter, 2016). On beans and indigenous foodways, see Rayna Green, "Mother Corn and the Dixie Pig: Native Food in the Native South," in *The Larder: Food Studies Methods from the American South*, ed. John T. Edge, Elizabeth S. D. Engelhardt, and Ted Ownby (Athens: University of Georgia Press, 2013), 155–65.

6. Glenn Brown, interview by Abigail Huggins, June 6, 2016.

7. Debbie Adams, interview by Abigail Huggins, August 8, 2016.

8. Bennett and Colette Quillen, interview by Abigail Huggins, July 18, 2016.

9. Don Maggard, interview by Abigail Huggins, July 21, 2016.

10. Brown interview.

11. Gwen and Mable Johnson, interview by Abigail Huggins, July 18, 2016.

12. For more on the impact of electricity and refrigeration on Appalachian foodways, see Lora Smith, "Electric Jell-O: Refrigeration Brought the Jiggle to Rural Appalachia," *Gravy* 58 (Winter 2016), https://www.southernfoodways.org/electric-jell-o/.

Chapter 6

My Great-Grandmother Is a Cherokee ...

Annette Saunooke Clapsaddle

"FOOD'S ready. Get in line." There are no more angst-inducing words in the southern lexicon. Until this announcement, we've all been just polite enough to hold out until the food is blessed; but now comes the moment when we have to decide who leads the charge to the buffet line. Who deserves sustenance first translates into who is valued most, and then that question is further simmered to a sticky reduction of what's really important: who gets the inaugural scoop of corn pudding?

For two communities that have long-shared traditions, there is also no scene more exemplary of the cultural difference between southern Appalachian and Cherokee social practices. If I am attending a small-town family reunion in rural Western North Carolina, my eight- and four-year-old sons jerk me from my seat, while blue-haired ladies shove precariously balanced Styrofoam plates into each of my hands so that the boys can make their picky selections of the spread—likely limited to beige carbohydrates. If I am in Cherokee, I settle in to wait, or, if need be, join the serving crew. This is because the first to be served in Cherokee (and generally among Native people) are the elders. Other gatherings prioritize parents providing food for their children, a practice not uncommon at restaurants when servers ask if we would like our children's orders brought out before our food is ready. This difference not only highlights the perceived order of human importance but also underscores a differentiation between helping the vulnerable and honoring the venerable.

This periodically causes confusion for my children, who cannot understand why near strangers are pulling them to the front of a line and haphazardly eroding the sanctity of their would-be dessert vessel with the likes of runny casseroles and greasy chicken legs, all while their mother flails behind, helpless, shouting dietary recommendations and reminders to "use your manners." It is disorienting for us all. In practical terms, it is also frustrating to have a toddler running around a fellowship hall, weaving in and out of wheelchairs and walkers, looking for a way to expend his sugar-fueled energy because he has already finished eating before the adults have even begun.

For the Cherokee, being at the head of the line is not simply an honor that acknowledges years spent on this earth. Whether they are serving as a *headman* or *headwoman* in a traditional dance, or linking arms in the front of the picket line, Cherokee elders are there to lead. They are the example we strive to follow—in celebrating or in fighting. They are to be seen, heard, *and* followed. Opportunities for gratitude and leadership are equally communicated in Cherokee culture. While McDonald's offers seniors discounted coffee out of respect for an aging population, the Cherokee Tribal Council offers elders seats on influential committees and boards out of reverence for their experiences.

Cherokee culture also has a process for recognizing those individuals who uphold its traditions and ideals through a life of integrity and care for others. To be named a *Beloved Woman* or *Beloved Man* signifies the highest honor the tribe can award. Such a title cannot be earned through singular acts or political favor. Though similar to a lifetime achievement award, the honor marks a beginning rather than an end. It signifies to the entire tribe that this person walks a path we should all strive to follow. While the title can be awarded posthumously, living Beloved Women and Men lead cultural preservation and revitalization efforts well into their eighties and nineties. Recently, Beloved Woman Myrtle Driver translated a chapter from Charles Frazier's *Thirteen Moons* and E. B. White's *Charlotte's Web* (to be used by immersion school students) into the Cherokee language, and Beloved Man Jerry Wolfe works full-time at the Museum of the Cherokee Indian to share knowledge and stories with visitors. He's a local celebrity, generously contributing to the education of both Cherokee and non-Cherokee.

Traditionally, it is not uncommon for extended families in Cherokee communities to share households, co-raise children, and divide work. The elder, often female, head of the family oversees this complex organization and intertwining of relationships. For this reason, politicians will speak to the elders of a large family, understanding that their children and grandchildren will likely follow the matriarch's or patriarch's lead in the polling booth. This is also one reason why claiming to have a great-grandmother who is a Cherokee Indian princess will likely be met with an eye roll. You might have a grandmother who is Cherokee, but she was far too busy strengthening tribal democracy to be a princess.

My own grandmother served on the Tribal Council for over twenty years without missing a single meeting. One of my favorite stories of her senior leadership is of the time a younger councilman saw her across the street in a nearby town. When my grandmother acknowledged his presence by nodding to him, he immediately raised his hand as if to vote in accordance with her suggestion.

After all, that's how the exchange would have happened if they had been in the Council Chambers passing legislation.

Esteem for Cherokee elders is hard earned. They are tasked with being conduits of traditional lifeways. As keepers of medicinal, spiritual, and cultural knowledge, elders are the storytellers who meticulously impart information through shared experience. These teachers commit to endless hours of mentoring that requires the student to be persistent and the teacher to be patient. The passing along of sacred knowledge can take years. Cherokee language translators are the most sought-after experts for miles around. Their hours are long and arduous, but our language's entire future rests heavily on their shoulders. For this reason, these native speakers are constant fixtures at events, at workshops, or in schools—days, nights, and weekends. They are often long past the average age of retirement, but they have only increased their service to their community over the years. Regardless of expertise, Cherokee elders are expected to serve in whatever capacity they can. In modern times, fewer elders possess traditional knowledge of medicinal plants and language, but that in no way diminishes their roles in our communities. There are new wisdoms to impart, additional familial complications, and the increasing urgency for protecting core Cherokee values, including spirituality, group harmony, strong individual character, strong connection to land stewardship, honoring the past, educating children, and possessing a sense of humor. It is a job, a responsibility, and an honor to be a Cherokee elder.

So at our next Cherokee gathering, as my stomach growls and my children beg to get just one warm yeast roll, it becomes my responsibility to show them that patience is the first lesson they will be learning from their elders that day. The next lesson is that they will only inherit what is left for them by the generation that precedes them.

Poem

Terrain

Crystal Wilkinson

the map of me can't be all hills and mountains even though i've
been geographically rural and country all my life. the twang in my
voice has moved downhill to the flat land a time or two. my taste
buds have exiled themselves from fried green tomatoes and rhubarb
for goats' milk and pine nuts. still i am haunted by home. i return
to old ground time and again, a homing black bird destined to
always return. i am a plain brown bag, oak and twig, mud pies and gut-
wrenching gospel in the throats of old tobacco brown men, when my
spine crooks even further toward my mother's i will continue to crave
the bulbous twang of wild shallots, the gamey familiarity of oxtails
and kraut boiling in a cast-iron pot. i toe-dive in all the rivers seeking
the whole of me, scout virtual african terrain trying to sift through

ancestral memories, but still i'm called back home through hymns sung by stout black women in large hats and flowered dresses. i can't say the landscape of me is all honeysuckle and clover cause there have always been mines in these lily-covered valleys. you have to risk the briar bush to reach the sweet dark fruit, and ain't no country woman all church and piney woods. there is pluck and cayenne pepper. there is juke joint gyrations in the young'un-bearing girth of this belly and these supple hips. all roads lead me back across the waters of blood and breast milk, from ocean, to river, to the lake, to the creek, to branch and stream, back to the sweet rain, to the cold water in the glass i drink when i thirst to know where i belong.

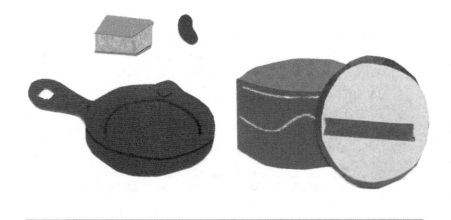

Chapter 7

Eating to Go

Courtney Balestier

AFTER MY grandmother died, my mother started finding pennies everywhere. On the floor of her house in West Virginia, in her car, places where minutes or hours before there had not been pennies. The work of my grandmother, she believed. I didn't doubt it; I don't need to be convinced of the universe's potential for mystery and, anyway, as a writer, I'm fond of symbolism. So I couldn't overlook, years later, being confronted with my own message, a piece of family DNA so specific and (I'd thought) so idiosyncratic that all I could do when it was placed in my hands was laugh: a Cool Whip container full of soup beans.

Old Cool Whip containers, originally purchased to make one or another dessert, were my grandmother's preferred method of kitchen storage, and more often than not they were storing navy beans. Raised in a coal mining camp in Appalachian Pennsylvania, she always had beans ready, and she was always sending people into her kitchen to get themselves something to eat (their hunger often irrelevant). I'm not saying that Appalachian grandmothers have the market on generosity cornered; I am saying that it's not a coincidence that the person who handed me that subsequent Cool Whip container of beans—even though she did so in metro Detroit— was also an Appalachian grandmother.

We talk so much about work when we talk about Appalachia: talk about ourselves as hardworking, hear ourselves described as hard workers. Often these conversations are about men, usually coal miners, who, of course, worked and work hard.[1] But there are many kinds of work. There is also the work of women like my grandmother, the work of making and sustaining the homes that, together, make a place. This work is harder to see. But that's what this is all about, before we get to the Cool Whip container, to the reason that this Appalachian grandmother and I were in Detroit in the first place: work, in all its forms, and the communities we build around it. Wherever it takes us.

The Hillbilly Highway, the mid-twentieth-century migration in which seven million Appalachians left their economically stagnant mountains for the factory towns and cities of the North—Akron, Detroit, Chicago—was a path to work.[2] In the 1940s, the Hillbilly Highway migration was spurred by the war effort and its need for tanks, planes, and armory. In Detroit, many Appalachians worked at Willow Run, a military bomber plant constructed in nearby Ypsilanti, and lived in the temporary community, Willow Village, constructed to house temporary workers. By the 1950s and '60s, the driving engine behind migration was mechanization in the coal mines, which had dramatically reduced jobs, and then Appalachians in Detroit got jobs in the auto industry, at plants like Dodge Main that no longer employ many people or no longer exist. The flow of traffic into Detroit was somewhat obvious: Henry Ford already owned coal mines in Kentucky and West Virginia, and northern companies had begun recruiting in the South, whose workers they believed to be unlikely to unionize, which is another way of saying to be unlikely to recognize the value of their work, the worth of the bodies that performed it.[3] At both of the Hillbilly Highway's apogees, then, it was about the work of brawn, the work that bosses are always telling Appalachians we do so well.

Jobs were everywhere in Detroit then—children of the migration have told me stories about people getting hired the day they got to town—but people missed their homes. As Appalachian scholar Ronald D. Eller wrote in *Uneven Ground: Appalachia since 1945*, "It was not uncommon on Friday nights in the 1950s to find the highways flowing south from Akron, Dayton, Cincinnati, Detroit and Chicago filled with Appalachian migrants heading to West Virginia, Kentucky and Tennessee." I imagine some of these people had intentions similar to Detroit-area labor union president Lloyd T. Jones, when he said of his own move to Detroit from Ford's Kentucky coal mines, in a 1940 Ford Radio Talk, "I knew it would be easy to save up a couple of thousand dollars in a year or so, go back home, put up a gas station, and then just coast along on the station's profits." But Jones stayed, of course. *Appalachian Odyssey*, an academic study of the migration, found that most others did, too.[4]

Work is also what brought me to Detroit sixty years later, not from my native West Virginia but from New York, my home for the previous eight years and where my husband and I were living when a Detroit university offered him a professorship. I did not know about the Hillbilly Highway then, but now, when I imagine the Detroit my Appalachian forebears arrived in—the Paris of the Midwest, Motown, the true Motor City—visions of urbane glamour take over. Women with fur hand muffs and men in hats driving cars with the muscular elegance of sharks. Martha and the Vandellas and the Four Tops playing everywhere, nowhere, all the time, indivisible from the air itself. It's a place of energy, a city of industry and an industrious city. A place of work.

The Detroit I arrived in, late in the summer of 2013, still carried the sour smell of the city's bankruptcy, the nation's first. The August air was thick and unfriendly and people shuffled silent streets, sometimes walking in the middle of the road, sometimes steering motorized wheelchairs, and I wondered why anyone had stayed. This was a naive question, but I asked it because I had not stayed in my home, and in not staying I had expressed a certain ambivalence toward the threat of defeat, a certain refusal of responsibility for that outcome or any other. That's how it had begun, for me, the studying of my steps but not the retracing of them, the questioning whether some of us need to love some things that way, at a remove. Though my exile is self-imposed, I still feel the length of its tether every day, in the choices I make and do not make.

IT'S a bit on the nose, but I live now in the same neighborhood that many southerners, including Appalachians, did when they arrived here: the Cass Corridor. Except now they call it Midtown, to take the stink off the area's notoriety for drugs and prostitution. Here, southern newcomers lived in apartment buildings, some of them grand, "absolutely gorgeous apartments" that "they maintained very well." Carole Baker, a lifelong Detroiter, tells me this one morning in her bright living room in Woodbridge, a neighborhood of beautiful old homes separated from the Cass Corridor by the John C. Lodge Freeway, the M-10, one of several built in the 1950s and '60s in an era of highway construction that displaced or dissected numerous inner-city populations, especially African American ones.[5]

I met Baker when I was looking for Nancy McNiven-Glenn, a longtime Detroiter and native North Carolinian whose father brought the family up when he got work in the war factories. Nancy used to own Nancy Whiskey, a legendary bar in the North Corktown neighborhood of Detroit, which also used to have a notable southern white population. The women are close friends. Both interacted with many Appalachian newcomers back then. They said the migrants were religious and clannish (another familiar adjective) but quick to help anyone, sharing food and child-rearing duties when someone had to go to work.

McNiven-Glenn laughed remembering the camaraderie she shared with a Kentucky-born bar owner in the neighborhood, where a fight would break out once or twice a week. One day, he called her up. "He said, 'Nancy!'"—she mimicked a high-pitched twang—"'I'm about starvin' myself and I can't go off and leave this bar. What'd you cook for lunch?' I said, 'I'll be right there with it.'" That's the way it was in both directions, she said. "They were right there for you; it didn't matter." Baker agreed; she would employ southerners to fix her properties, because they were hard workers and she could trust them.

Then I asked what kind of food the southerners cooked, and Baker lit up. "Oh, I love cornbread and beans. Cornbread dressing was my *favorite*. Anyone who was southern, I'd ask them, 'Please make me cornbread dressing.'"

Cornbread seems to have gone over big here. An Appalachian man named Powell Conley told me that when he was growing up in Willow Village, the bomber plant housing near Ypsilanti, a neighbor woman used to come by at suppertime and eat so much cornbread that his mother started baking her a separate batch. Conley's father moved the family from Salyersville, Kentucky, in 1951, when Conley was eight. I met him in 2016, at the best answer to the question of what became of the Appalachian migration to Detroit: the meeting hall of the Kentuckians of Michigan.

The Kentuckians of Michigan have been meeting since 1960, gathering Appalachian transplants from Kentucky, West Virginia, Tennessee, and Virginia. Its members throw Christmas, Halloween, and St. Patrick's Day parties; knit blankets and hats for local hospitals and soldiers serving overseas; and host bluegrass and country musicians from around the country. The Kentuckians' major event, though, has always been its annual picnic. In 1963, ten thousand people attended. Last year, it was closer to three hundred. Most of these folks are in their sixties or older, and most of them haven't been home—*home* home—in a few years, since the last of their people died. The younger generations, a few tell me, aren't as interested.

But the Kentuckians keep going, in a meeting house down a wooded gravel road best driven slowly, the kind of drive that reminds you how rural Michigan can be (and it can get more rural still). Their hall would feel familiar to anyone who, like me, grew up being dragged to dances and dinners at the VFW or the Elks Lodge. The walls are covered in wood paneling and memorabilia, including the state flag of Kentucky and a framed and yellowed *National Enquirer* article from the 1970s that claimed Pikeville, Kentucky, boasted one millionaire per every sixty residents ("The energy crunch has transformed this poverty-ridden coal community into a town of back-slapping millionaires").[6] Here, the Kentuckians hold weekly bluegrass nights with live music and soup bean suppers, prepared in an old but spotless kitchen that is staffed, at any given moment, by two to six women and zero cookbooks.

When I visited, there were beans simmering on the stove in a pressure cooker and ham warming in the oven. They prepared green beans and salad, mixed mashed potatoes from potato flakes, and readied store-bought desserts. But what's important is not that some conveniences were taken but that two specific conveniences were not: The cornbread came from the cooks' homes, in the shape of well-loved cast-iron skillets, in such quantities that I was sent home with an entire round, untouched through dinner. And along the top shelf of the Kentuckians' kitchen sat large holiday tins of the type that probably once held specialty popcorn but were now full of dried beans, their contents scrawled on the front in marker: white beans, brown beans, pinto beans.

The first time I attended a Kentuckians' event was September 2016, soon after they resumed from a seasonal break. As I sat eating my beans and cornbread, kielbasa and sauerkraut, fried cabbage, mashed potatoes, and green beans, I overheard a man tell a woman named Carlotta Lowe that this was his first soup bean meal since the Kentuckians had wrapped up their previous season.

"Oh, honey," Carlotta said to the man. After a pause, something else occurred to her: Those weren't soup beans, she said to the man; they were great northern beans. Soup beans are brown. The man told her that, in his family, soup beans were white. (They were in mine, too.) There is a sense in which this distinction does not matter and a sense in which it says everything about the migration north: the color of my soup beans versus the color of your soup beans only matters when we are both in a third place, talking about our soup beans.

Lowe, from Pikeville, Kentucky—she had shown me the *Enquirer* article with pride—has an ornery smile that makes you want in on the mischief, the come-sit-here-by-me type. When I did go sit by her, at a table full of the women who had prepared dinner, I learned that she was also that creature that Appalachia produces so well: a storyteller. She led the table in sharing stories of home. The funerals that used to be held right in the house, how there would be netting over the body to keep the flies away and everyone would sit with the deceased overnight out of respect. How no one locked their doors—if somebody knocked, Lowe told me, they were trying to sell you something. Joy Sammut, the group's secretary, explained that her brothers used to "sheet" her bed: pull the bottom of the sheet up to the top so that, when she got in, she got tangled up. Lowe said her father and aunt used to pull similar pranks on each other in her youth, sneaking into one another's homes while they were out, taking food out of the fridge or dishes out of the cupboards, moving rugs, turning down beds. One woman was crocheting small scouring pads for washing dishes as the evening passed, and after a bit she tossed me one, though I hadn't asked for it. And then I moved to leave and was inundated with leftovers, the centerpiece of which was that Cool Whip container of leftover soup beans, which I photographed as soon as I got home to show my cousins.

My grandmother was my first step in embracing Appalachia, though I didn't know that's what I was doing. Her beans, making them on my own in New York and Detroit, making them before and after her death, were my first understanding of communion. She was a devout Catholic, Mary Hidock, so perhaps she would be disappointed to know that. But while I knew plenty of warm, joyful gatherings around her family table, I found a specific truth away from it, the same one I encountered at the Kentuckians' hall, which is that one only comprehends the spiritual resonance of food when something is missing. To be at a remove confronts one with a choice; one has to work to adapt what one knows to where one is, to who is not there with one. One has to decide whether to let that spirit live or die. One has to pledge oneself back to oneself, the way that, in the endless Easter masses of my childhood, the priest would ask us to pledge ourselves back to God.

AT the Kentuckians' hall, I met people raised in metro Detroit who speak with southern accents, so surrounded were they by Appalachians. One of them is Burl Stevens, who's from Wyandotte, a neighboring town, but whose parents came north from eastern Kentucky. I met Burl on the porch the same night I met Conley. I had come with questions about the Hillbilly Highway, and Conley was suspicious of most of them.

"Unfortunately, the questions haven't changed since the '40s and '50s," Conley said. "Writers are not the most . . . what's the word, Burl?"

"Don't ask me," Burl said.

Conley settled on "dependable." "Nearly all of us that came up here could read and write," he said. I told him I assumed as much. "Well, many don't," he said. "'Buncha dumb hillbillies.'" Appalachians were just doing "what people did for years and years before," he said. "They went where the work was. It's no different now." Conley met people here from all over the country, and yet, he said, writers could only ever find Kentuckians and West Virginians. I asked what questions I should be asking—what the flip side of that story is.

"The flip side is the humanity of it," he said. "Those of us who came here weren't any different than the ones that were already here. We might have talked a little different, we might eat a little different"—he paused, laughed—"We did teach 'em how to eat up here."

I heard nothing harsher than this "buncha dumb hillbillies" remark from the dozen or so Appalachians I spoke with about their moves north, all of them white Baby Boomers and most of them Kentucky natives, but the written record of the Hillbilly Highway is not nearly as compassionate. An article by Louis Adamic, published in 1934 in *The Nation*, referred to the incoming Appalachians as "white trash or a little better." These "hill-billies," Adamic wrote, "with their extremely low standard of living and lack of acquaintance with modern plumbing, are looked down upon by all but the most intelligent local workers, both native and foreign born; they are despised also—indeed, mainly—because they take employment away from the old-time automotive workers." Adamic, a cultural critic, was reacting to Detroit employers who equated Appalachians with mechanical aptitude and a strong work ethic and the resulting rising tensions he witnessed in the city.[7]

In a *Harper's* article from twenty years later entitled "The Hillbillies Invade Chicago," writer Albert Votaw used similar language to describe "these farmers, miners and mechanics from the mountains and meadows of the mid-South" as "clannish, proud, disorderly, untamed to urban ways," confounding "all notions of racial, religious and cultural purity." In Cincinnati and Chicago, workshops were held to explain mountain people's "peculiar ways." The Council of the Southern Mountains—the home team, as it were—sponsored speakers to address city professionals about the "strangers" entering their communities. A survey by Detroit's Wayne State University, taken just after World War II, asked, "What people in Detroit are undesirable?" Respondents ranked "poor Southern whites; hillbillies, etc.," second, just below criminals.[8]

Because of the way America continues to speak and think about Appalachia, as if it were a particularly difficult children's puzzle, none of this surprises me. But it's interesting to note that, according to the editors of *Appalachian Odyssey*, all rural migrants moving around the country in the mid-twentieth century—Appalachians, southern black and white sharecroppers, Mexican Americans, Puerto Ricans—experienced a migration more characteristically foreign than domestic. They faced struggles obtaining employment, housing, and education, and experienced "various forms of prejudice and discrimination." It is worth stressing again that the sampling of Appalachian migrants I met were white. Discrimination faced by oppressed racial minorities is incomparable, and the deep, complex research into this history is beyond the scope of this essay. White Appalachians, even those who faced discrimination, still had advantages—including those resulting from racist policies, like housing discrimination—that black, Latino, and other migrants did not.[9] In this nation that crows about its immigrant roots, othering is a time-honored tradition. Has there ever been a tolerable time to be the other, to not feel the force of our American heart's contempt for the other parts of its body?

UNLIKE the vibrant immigrant communities around Detroit known for their restaurants—the Polish and, increasingly, Bangladeshi city of Hamtramck; the working-class neighborhood of Southwest, or Mexicantown; Dearborn, with its significant Arab community, largely Lebanese and Assyrian—there are no neighborhoods where one goes to eat Appalachian cuisine in restaurants. The food is shared, it seems, in private; even the Kentuckians' hall, while its bluegrass nights are open to the public, is essentially a clubhouse. Wagner, Obermiller, and Turner agree, writing, "Many of these migrants and their descendants overcame the social and economic barriers they found in the cities either by assimilating or by becoming bicultural, that is, becoming adept at normative speech, dress and behavior in public while retaining Appalachian cultural characteristics in their personal lives."[10] In the landscape of Detroit, aside from the old suffixed nicknames of the suburbs where many Appalachians settled—Taylortucky (Taylor), Ypsitucky (Ypsilanti), Hazeltucky (Hazel Park)—it would seem Appalachians blended into the native flora and fauna. What the Hillbilly Highway produced here, perhaps, was something more specific than Appalachian Americans. It created Appalachian Detroiters.

When I began researching Appalachian cuisine early in my writing career, I was told that some people don't classify it as a cuisine at all, so rudimentary was its style and so maligned were its participants. An academic told me this, sympathetically. But who are those people, and why do they get to decide? Is it because we've always been too busy working to draw those lines ourselves? I can't imagine what midcentury Appalachians would have said to the idea that their bowl of soup beans and slice of cornbread wasn't characteristic of a specific region, didn't evoke the tastes and flavors of the mountains. What the women who made those beans and that cornbread would have said. What my grandmother would have said had someone walked into her home—the house where her husband was born, where she raised four children while he bagged groceries and sold men suits—and uttered a statement like that. "Did you eat yet?," probably.

WILLOW Village, where Powell Conley's family lived, was constructed by the Federal Public Housing Administration to address the severe housing crisis caused by Willow Run's glut in production. Willow Village was always meant to be temporary, and so it was. Today all that employee housing is gone, replaced by modest homes with vinyl siding. You can drive around, as I have, under brittle winter sunlight by the guide of a historical map, but you won't find much but sites that used to be one thing and are now something else: schools, apartment complexes, single-story homes that you imagine never come all the way clean. The only thing that remains—besides the factory itself, which stands, slowly crumbling, behind a locked gate at a small airport—is one of the churches that Henry Ford built and named after his mother and mother-in-law, the chapels of Martha and Mary. (It was moved a few miles away from its original location.) I wonder if the Appalachian workers found this strange— moving to a settlement so thoroughly constructed, for the purposes of their labor, of its own mythology—or if by this point they thought little of rich men inventing icons for them to worship.

Something about Willow Run pains me, and I recognize that this pain is probably undue, because it was a place where people who wanted jobs got them, a place where those people's families were fed. Perhaps it's the question that the ghost of Willow Run leaves for me. Why does it feel like we Appalachians are yoked to company towns? What was the difference, really, in trading King Coal for Henry Ford? But these are not my questions to answer, perhaps not even my questions to ask in the first place, because when I left Appalachia I meant never to go back. And yet, I can't help but feel offended by the temporary nature of Willow Village, erected and razed like a traveling circus, that stupid church left bright white against the low gray belly of the Michigan sky. *You were here,* the place says to me now, *but then we erased you.*

THE Hillbilly Highway was about a move for opportunity; my husband and I moved for opportunity, too. But to move to Detroit these days is often about a different kind of opportunism, the kind that involves $500 houses and theories of postapocalyptic utopia, visions built on bones picked clean. And so I understand why there is a similar but different air of antagonism toward newcomers now: the "Don't Brooklyn My Detroit" T-shirts, the media lecturing of nonnatives (a local author's book is called *How to Live In Detroit without Being a Jackass*), the simmering battle of gentrification, the long-standing racial tensions that battle brings to the surface.

I sympathize with this. (I came to Detroit from Brooklyn, after all, the borough responsible for the subway-tiled, air plant-adorned aesthetic of most mid-major cities.) I would be angry as well if outsiders referred to my home as a blank slate, as if I were not still there. I would be angry if they misjudged it, the way I am angry when people misjudge Appalachia. Like the concierge at the downtown Detroit hotel, when I said I was getting married in my native West Virginia, who asked if I was marrying my cousin. Or the *Detroit Free Press* reporter who, the year I moved here, tweeted an incest joke about my home state that I still think about, my chest burning at its casual violence. Or the community leader (not a born Detroiter, I should note) in a neighborhood of historical Appalachian immigration who spoke his stereotypes matter-of-factly as my jaw clenched tighter, assuring me that it wasn't merely prejudice but also, of all things, scholarly opinion.

It's so striking to me, in these moments, how West Virginia, the piece of Appalachia that I come from, and Detroit have taken different routes to the same place: to a state of being so unseen and so misunderstood, of watching outsiders look at us from different angles yet always take the same picture. Both of my homes even romanticize their fortitude against this gaze with slogans: Detroit Versus Everybody, Mountaineers Are Always Free. We are so different and so similar, on the rotted foundations of our mono-economies. I come from one land of the hardworking, neglected other and I live in another one now, which is like being sent to stay with a distant relative: the family resemblance might not be strong, but it's there. We are workers, all of us. We did the work, and then the work no longer needed doing, at least not by us. But we are here still.

I said to a lifelong Detroiter once, a woman whose wisdom about my new home I've come to rely on, that I thought some (not all) of the cries of gentrification in the city were misapplied—that, sometimes, it wasn't a case of a mom-and-pop shop being pushed out for a luxury retailer or residents being forced out by inflated rents. Sometimes, it seemed to me, development happened where there was nothing to displace. You have to understand what was there before, she said. The ghosts of that Detroit, a Detroit that she loved, were being displaced. *You were here, but then we erased you.* I don't know if I agree with her; places have to adapt to change as much as people do. But I empathize.

I have been in Detroit for five years now. Like my home, it often makes me angry; like my home, my presence in it sometimes feels joyful, sometimes impossible. But, like Appalachians before me, I have settled here; I understand the tiny ways that a strange place becomes home a bit more each day, through sheer familiarity and repetition, without your doing a thing. It has been fourteen years since I lived in West Virginia. I don't know if I ever will again. I don't know how long I will be here, either. Some days, my presence here feels as inevitable as that Cool Whip container of beans; other days, I drive down the highway and want to keep going.

NOTES

1. Even here, though, we must be careful: as synonymous as coal is with Appalachia, I've spoken to expatriated Appalachians who grew up hearing their fathers vow to never work a day underground.

2. For more on the Hillbilly Highway, see Thomas J. Sugrue, *The Origins of the Urban Crisis: Race and Inequality in Postwar Detroit* (Princeton, NJ: Princeton University Press, 1996); Chad Berry, *Southern Migrants, Northern Exiles* (Urbana: University of Illinois Press, 2000); James N. Gregory *The Southern Diaspora: How the Great Migrations of Black and White Southerners Transformed America* (Chapel Hill: University of North Carolina Press, 2005).

3. "Henry Ford Develops Kentucky County," *New York Times*, June 20, 1925; "Ford Buys West Virginia Coal Property," *Wall Street Journal*, November 16, 1922. It's too broad an assumption to claim all southerners were inoculated against unionization, but it's an especially puzzling one regarding Appalachians: West Virginia had already gone through its mine wars for workers' rights and union recognition, including 1921's Battle of Blair Mountain, the largest US insurrection since the Civil War and the largest labor uprising in American history. Thomas Klug, a history professor at Marygrove College who kindly shared materials here, told me that the United Mine Workers was a model industrial union, integral to the success of steel, auto, and rubber worker unions. Further, Detroit union champions Roy and Walter Reuther were natives of Wheeling, West Virginia, and southern women workers from mining areas were crucial in the union drive to organize female employees at Detroit's Ternstedt General Motors parts plant. Ruth Meyerowitz, "Organizing the United Automobile Workers: Women Workers at the Ternstedt General Motors Parks Plant," in *Women, Work and Protest: A Century of U.S. Women's Labor History*, ed. Ruth Milkman (Boston: Routledge, 1985), 242–43.

4. Ronald D. Eller, *Uneven Ground: Appalachia since 1945* (Lexington: University Press of Kentucky, 2008), 22; "Text of UAW-CIO Radio Address of Lloyd T. Jones," July 25, 1940, Box 1 Ford Radio Talks, 1940,

Edward Levinson Collection, Archives of Labor and Urban Affairs, Walter P. Reuther Library, Wayne State University, Detroit, MI; Phillip J. Obermiller, Thomas E. Wagner, and E. Bruce Tucker, eds., *Appalachian Odyssey: Historical Perspectives on the Great Migration* (Westport, CT: Praeger, 2000).

5. Sugrue, *Origins of the Urban Crisis,* 106.

6. Quotation from the *National Enquirer* profile of Pikeville, Kentucky, from notes in the author's possession.

7. Louis Adamic, "The Hill-Billies Come to Detroit," *The Nation,* February 13, 1934, 177, https://socialwelfare.library.vcu.edu/eras/great-depression/hill-billies-come-detroit-1934/. On employer assumptions, see Thomas E. Wagner, Phillip J. Obermiller, and Bruce Tucker, "Introduction," in *Appalachian Odyssey,* xii.

8. Albert N. Votaw, "The Hillbillies Invade Chicago," *Harper's Magazine,* February 1958, 64; Phillip J. Obermiller and Thomas E. Wagner, "'Hands-Across-the-Ohio': The Urban Initiatives of the Council of the Southern Mountains, 1954–1971," in *Appalachian Odyssey,* 121–40; John Hartigan Jr., "'Disgrace to the Race': *Hillbillies* and the Color Line in Detroit," in *Appalachian Odyssey,* 147–50.

9. Wagner, Obermiller, and Tucker, "Introduction," in *Appalachian Odyssey,* xiii. For more on these issues, see Sugrue, *Origins of the Urban Crisis;* Barbara Ellen Smith, "De-Gradations of Whiteness: Appalachia and the Complexities of Race," *Journal of Appalachian Studies* 10, nos. 1–2 (Spring/Fall 2004): 38–57.

10. Wagner, Obermiller, and Tucker, "Introduction," in *Appalachian Odyssey,* xiv.

Chapter 8

What You Find and What You Lose
When You Seek a New Home

Michael Croley

THE WEEK it opened, cars in the drive-thru curled around the building in a kind of steel embrace, and at school we asked one another, "Have you been yet?" There was no need to say the name. We knew. Taco Bell had come to Corbin, bringing with it the world, it seemed. That first Saturday, the cheerleaders held a fund-raising event there, decked out in pleated skirts and red T-shirts tied into knots above their belly buttons.

We already had plenty of fast food joints. There was McDonald's, Wendy's, Arby's, Hardee's (where the old men took their coffee in the mornings), and, of course, Kentucky Fried Chicken, founded in my hometown. But we grew up with those; they were as much a part of the terrain of Corbin as the water tower sitting near the middle of town. I saw them too often to connect them to their larger corporate offices and outposts in other parts of the country and world.

Of course, there was a casualty. As soon as we all started "running for the border," Taco-Tico's days were numbered. This small regional chain also offered bad tacos, but the only reason any of us went there was because it occupied prime real estate next to the movie theater. Thousands of middle school and high school students must have walked through its glass doors before and after movies. How many first kisses took place in those high-backed wooden booths? How many fistfights were started in its parking lot? Joints rolled in the restrooms? Taco-Tico was a hub of teenage angst and culture, our own *American Graffiti*. Taco Bell shut it down for good.

Corbin always felt isolated, even though we were right on I-75. There was this sense we had to get out of Corbin to see the real America, which was the country that existed in commercials and sitcoms and had nothing to do with our own small hometown. On a church youth trip to New Mexico during my sophomore year, some of us bought Baja sweaters and hoodies, only to feel out of place when we wore them on our return. I was surprised two years later when those sweaters finally became popular in Corbin, proving we were always behind the national trends.

Taco Bell's arrival in 1995 wasn't the only change taking hold. A Walmart was coming to town—another example of the world coming to Corbin. And the internet was coming to life. During my morning study hall, I entered our library and used a dial-up connection to get online and access the now-defunct Webcrawler search engine. I don't remember what I was looking for, but suddenly a world that had always seemed hidden to me, the unnameable and unknowable things I thought I was missing out on as a boy growing up in Corbin, were at my fingertips. I would call my brother Tim, then in graduate school, who had access to fast internet on campus, and he would tell me things I could search for, talk me through email, and teach me about the power of the web.

As a teenager, I worked a series of odd jobs for spending money, often with my friend Gregg, who had gone to high school with my brother. We mowed yards together, installed insulation in attics, worked in a vinyl-siding warehouse, and hauled freight. Except for the mowing, the other men we met performing these jobs were all in their twenties, just like Gregg. They were trying to make their way into life and adulthood. Some married; some on the verge. I was an outlier, and in jobs like these, particularly during the all-day mowing stints and the warehouse work, I quickly learned that our days revolved around lunch. Lunch was a forty-five-minute break with air-conditioning, a way for the body to slow down and find a rhythm that wasn't hurried—or harried—and regain some footing, mentally and physically. Gregg and I began our mornings planning where we would go come lunchtime. We usually alternated between Wendy's and Arby's and, occasionally, we'd hit the Sonic Drive-In.

One day, in line at Wendy's, Gregg and I ran into a friend of my brother's from high school, a guy I often played pick-up basketball with at the Rec Center. He was an industrial plumber—still a young man, twenty-five at most. He had come in with his coworkers from a job site, his face dusted with grime and dirt, wearing ripped jeans and steel-toed boots. He shook my hand, and what struck me was not the roughness of it, but its thickness. He had been rangy as a teenager. A stint in the marines made him stouter, but his hand had a meatiness to it that wasn't so much strength as it was like scar tissue. "How you doing?" I asked. And with a weariness I have never forgotten, he replied, "Let me tell you something, Mikey. Don't ever get a job where you have to use your body." He had jackhammered a cement walkway all morning, and his ears were still ringing and his body still shaking. Whenever I saw him after that, at the gym, or someplace in town, I'd ask if he worked the jackhammer that day, fearing his answer would be yes.

One afternoon when I was seventeen, I came home from the vinyl-siding warehouse pissed off and tired. I had to get to an evening football practice. My mom was in the kitchen, up to her wrists in egg roll filling, flecks of cabbage against her skin, the house smelling of garlic and pepper. She asked what was wrong. I told her I had loaded an entire twenty-four-foot truck by myself that day because Gregg had been gone and our coworker was too lazy to help. I pulled a hundred boxes out of their racks over my head and then shouldered them twenty yards to the truck. The boxes were sixteen feet long and weighed seventy-five pounds apiece. I complained to my mother about my coworker's poor work ethic, how tired I was, how much I still had left to do in the day, but she stopped me cold. "Some people spend their whole lives in jobs like that. You're doing it for one summer."

Unlike my friends, I never said aloud that I was going to get out of Corbin and never come back. Even then, I knew it was a cliché to hate the place you're from. Plus, I didn't want to leave. For a time, I thought I would go off for college but then I'd be back. I said as much to Mom one day in the car, and the look she gave me was so withering, I thought she might run us into a guardrail to wake me up. "I moved eight thousand miles away from my family," she said. "I think you can move away from Corbin."

My mother met my father when he was stationed in Korea. He'd offered himself up to fight in the Vietnam War, but the government sent him to Korea. When they came to the States together, they lived in Phoenix, then Toledo, then Harlan County, then the countryside of Whitley County where my father had grown up, and then they finally settled in Corbin. For a long time, I was both sensitive and insecure about where I had grown up. I was wary of the headlines we made as a punchline for *The Tonight Show*, the way we were characterized in movies as dumb, backward, and incestuous. I knew that my accent, much thicker when I was a boy, marked me as different, even within Kentucky. To speak in my voice meant I often lost IQ points with strangers. To grow up in Corbin, half-Korean, often fending off racial slurs and teasing, meant to feel uncomfortable in the place I called home. I was torn between defending where I grew up, honoring the folks I knew and loved there, and feeling resentful and hurt by their provocations.

I had thought that Taco Bell was the world coming to us, but in the very house I grew up in, the very foods my mother fed me as a baby were part of a culinary tradition that went back to at least the thirteenth century. Korea's first cookbooks and texts on agriculture were written during the Joseon Dynasty in 1429. Our family ate hot pungent kimchi and chewy, jerky-like dried squid. My mother made special trips to the Korean grocery in Lexington an hour and a half away to buy fifty-pound bags of rice and jars of gochujang sauce that weren't in vogue as they are now. She'd come home and cook the rice and put it steaming hot into a leaf of romaine lettuce and then put a dab of the sauce on top for us, the heat of the sauce mixing with the steaming rice and cool, crisp lettuce. Often my brother and I would come home from school, open the packages of ramen she'd bought at the Korean market, and eat the hard discs of noodles raw, like an oversized cracker, sprinkling the seasoning powder over each bite. Neither of us knew until we were in college that ramen was considered cheap, mass-quantity food by Americans, because we had grown up with it as part of our daily diet.

To entice us to eat kimbap—rice rolled in seaweed—our mother cooked hot dogs and cut up slices to put in the rice. Her egg rolls strayed from purely vegetarian to contain pork, veal, and beef. They were as much an event for us as any Thanksgiving Day turkey or Christmas ham. One of my most vivid food memories is of going to my aunt and uncle's house for a catfish fry, to which my mother brought a large platter of bulgogi and steaming white rice. It wasn't strange to see it there among the spread of Appalachian food—potato salad, green beans cooked in pork fat, black-eyed peas. No one batted an eye; they just took their portion.

The summer before I turned sixteen, we went to Korea to visit our family there. I was determined to not be an ugly American and refuse the food put in front of me. The first morning at my aunt's house, a hot fish soup was brought out, along with rice and kimchi. The fish had been cooked whole, no filleting, and it was a dark-colored fish that looked like something that might be found floating on the surface of the creek out in the woods near home. I flinched. I might have fought a gag reflex. I ate the rice and kimchi. At lunch and then dinner, nearly the same meal was brought out again.

Two days of this, and I was jonesing so bad for a hamburger I couldn't stand it. By day five, my mother had gotten some peanut butter and jelly for Tim and me. That lasted us four days. On a trip through the Korean countryside, we stopped at a roadside travel plaza and rather than go for a steaming bowl of bibimbap, my mother bought two hamburgers for my brother and me, worried that we weren't eating enough. We had tried hard to be good sons, to be cultured, even, but we were losing. I still can't explain the texture or taste of those sorry hamburgers she bought us or the pained look on her face when she saw us bite down and fight to swallow. Her heart broke a little as she saw our contorted faces, but we told her it was fine. We bought another jar of peanut butter.

I wouldn't return to Korea again until I was thirty-two. This time it was just my mother and I. I ate everything set before me, though seven days in I went to a supermarket—the US model had finally made its way to Korea—and bought a sack of potatoes to make home fries each morning. Seoul, we found, had become more Americanized in the intervening years, flooded with Starbucks knock-offs, Dunkin' Donuts, and more KFCs than I had ever seen. The world had talked and traded. Korean food, which for centuries was peasant food, is now haute.

Sometimes we need our most important questions and observations to marinate and ferment before they turn into the ideas that shape and drive us toward whatever it is we are to become. I see now that in southeastern Kentucky, where I grew up, we were polyglots of Eastern and Western cuisine. If food is culture—and I think it is—then in this regard, and this one only, we were fluent in both. My mother taught herself to fry chicken in a cast-iron skillet and picked blackberries from the vine behind our house to make blackberry dumplings for dessert. At home, my brother and I ate the food from her youth and the food from our father's, and these became braided in our palates.

My mother assimilated out of necessity—there were not many Koreans in southeastern Kentucky—as well as out of admiration. She took in the language through soap operas, saying the melodrama helped her understand the meanings of the words. She eventually found her way to college and into the workforce. When we talk about immigration in this country, often we only talk about what the immigrant gains or, as is the case these days, what they "take." We don't consider what they have left behind; how there comes a day when they have lost their old ways, when they have blended so much that the beginning and the end of each separate culture are like train tracks in the distant horizon.

My mother once said to me, "I'll never really be an American, and I'm not really Korean anymore." I was in ninth grade at the time, and she had just returned from a three-year memorial service for her father in Korea. All sense of Korea being a home seemed to have disappeared for her. It has taken all the years from then until now for me to see that to grow up split, as I did, was to grow up not fully comprehending either of my cultures or the gnarly web of roots that tied them together. In a way, now, I feel as homeless as my mother. As a boy, I longed for the world outside the landscape of Corbin, represented in Baja sweaters and Taco Bell and the brand-new internet at my fingertips; and as a man, I still long to understand the place where I grew up, the place I have never returned to. It has left me, at times, adrift—wandering—wondering where I have come from, and where I will roam.

Chapter 9

Best Pal: Big on Hot Dogs, Hamburgers, and Quick Service

Emily Wallace

THE HUMONGOUS hot dog, hamburger, French fry, and soda sculptures affixed to Pal's Sudden Service drive-thru restaurants may seem somewhat out of their element where set against the mountainous landscapes of southwest Virginia and East Tennessee. But the absurd statues are as awe-inspiring as the region's natural lookouts, and are firmly rooted in contemporary Appalachia. Quick and affordable, hot dogs and their common fast-food companions have played important roles in feeding the region's workers. As West Virginia folklorist Emily Hilliard puts it, "Coal miners, steel workers, and other factory laborers needed a quick meal they could eat between or during shifts."[1] It's a point to emphasize—in the case of Pal's, on the side of a building.

Object-shaped structures, defined as programmatic architecture or "Ducks" (a term that references a mallard-ish building on Long Island), have a long and global history—from leafy garden topiaries in ancient Rome, to James V. Lafferty's "Lucy," a tin and wooden elephant-shaped building in South Atlantic City created in 1881, to John F. Williams's Bottle, a 64-foot-tall wooden building near Auburn, Alabama, built in 1924 and made to resemble a Nehi soda.[2] But the odd forms increased in popularity after World War II with fiberglass, as the material expanded in use beyond building boat and Corvette bodies to include those of men, horses, and pigs, as well as ice cream and other foodstuffs.[3] Across Florida in the 1980s, for instance, fiberglass created the magic shell for Twistee Treat buildings, which resembled the soft serve cones they sold. Around the same time in East Tennessee, Pal's began using it to fashion fast-food ornaments to attach to its drive-thru locations.

The chain got its start in 1956 when Fred "Pal" Barger opened a restaurant on Revere Street in his native Kingsport. By future standards, the original location is aesthetically a tad boring—a red-and-white tiled stand with Burgers and Shakes spelled out in neon above. In many ways, it mimicked 2-J, a walk-up hamburger joint in Austin, Texas, where Barger was stationed during the Korean War. Below a glitzy bun-like circle, a sign in front of 2-J advertised, "Over 6 million sold." Interested in creating something similar, Barger attended the National Restaurant Convention in Chicago, where, by happenstance, a man named Ray Kroc invited him down to Des Plaines, Illinois, to see what would become the first McDonald's franchise.

Like those at 2-J and McDonald's, Pal's early menu featured hamburgers, hot dogs, and French fries. But in 1990, the restaurant dubbed the latter Frenchie Fries—a goofy name that hints at Pal's penchant for the absurd. It's the side of the chain that put the figurine of an oversized hamburger-hefting man atop Pal's #2 on Lynn Garden Road, and the one that hired pop art duo Tony and Karen Barone to create a design for all future Pal's buildings.[4] As the *Los Angeles Times* once wrote of the artists, "In Venice, a town where the unusual is expected, the Barones (rhymes with spumoni) draw double takes wherever they go."[5]

Karen is known for wearing tall platforms and short, short neon dresses, while Tony tends to dress in all black. Sporting dozens of tiny braids and sheer bangs, Karen also paints large dark circles around her eyes, causing them to pop from her otherwise pale face. In the '80s, she created her own cosmetics line called Bar-one, which she sold at major department stores like Bloomingdale's, in addition to a SoHo shop that also bore her name.[6] Eventually, the Barones moved to a farm in East Tennessee—an area where their makeup was being created. And it's there that they met Pal Barger and got back to their initial business designing restaurants.

Before moving to New York, the Barones helped with several concept restaurants in Chicago, including Rich Melman's Jonathan Livingston Seafood and Lawrence of Oregano. Such endeavors led them to lecture at the National Restaurant Convention, where Barger heard them speak and became enamored of their work. Over dinner in Tennessee, he asked the two what they thought about reinventing the Pal's look. "We sketched out on a cocktail napkin basically a block building with a 24-foot hot dog," says Tony. "More is never enough with Karen, so she said, 'How about another idea?'" And he said, "No, this is *the* idea."[7]

Pal took the napkin drawing, which is framed on a wall at the Pal's corporate office, to architect Tony Moore, who built the first newly designed Pal's building in 1985. The result is something of a greasy stairwell to heaven, with giant fast-food sculptures resting on teal tile steps that climb up and above the drive-thru window. Initially, the idea was to get local first graders to vote on the color of the next Pal's exterior. So the first stair-step location was pastel green, the second, baby blue, and the third, not far from East Tennessee State University (ETSU), a pale pink.[8] "We do business by not hiding behind beige colors and oak floors," says Tony.[9] But the paints faded at different rates (there was also a kerfuffle when an ETSU professor was quoted in a local newspaper as saying the chain across the street was colored pink because the foods demanded a dose of Pepto-Bismol to wash them down), so Pal's decided to standardize with teal buildings. There are now twenty-nine locations—only the first few lack the tiered design and oversized foods—all within an eighty-mile radius of Kingsport. Pal's has kept it close to home, within what amounts to the bounds of a mustard glob on a map.

Each of the Pal's sculptures could be analyzed for its regional ties and significance. (Is the drink cup full of Dr. Enuf, Johnson City's cult soda, or Pal's Peachy Tea?) But it's the hot dog that's most emblematic. "The big-city dogs of Chicago, New York, and Philadelphia get most of the media attention," writes Fred Sauceman, a professor of Appalachian studies at ETSU, who created a documentary about red hot dogs along southwest Virginia's Lee Highway. "But the side streets and country backroads of southern Appalachia yield their own hot dog cuisine, a continuum from mustard-chili-onion loyalists to roasted red pepper revolutionaries."

In southwest Virginia, hot dogs were big industry themselves, as Lorenz Neuhoff Jr. began buying up local packing companies in the 1930s, manufacturing dogs under the name Neuhoff Incorporated. Later rebranded Valleydale Packers and advertised by a marching band of trombone- and drum-playing pigs, the company expanded across the Southeast and reported gross sales surpassing $100 million by 1958.[10] Lunch counters and sandwich stands doled out countless dogs. For its part, Pal's, which used Valleydale while the Bristol plant was in operation, estimates that it has sold more than 100 million hot dogs over its history.[11] As Sauceman tallies, "The unit cost of a red Valleydale hot dog is less than the unit cost of the bun you put it in. Those red hot dogs helped a lot of families through hard times, and they still do."[12] Of course, the same could be said of a thin-pattied burger, or a fried string of potato, which Pal's not only sells in gigantic quantities, but at rapid speed.

According to CEO Thom Crosby, the restaurant is more than three times as fast as its best competitor, handing a bag of hamburgers from the drive-thru to idling customers in an average of eighteen seconds during its lunch rush. "We look at when the wheels stop at the pick-up window to when they start moving again," says Crosby.[13] So for food that is fleeting (beyond the drive-thru, a hot dog is at most five bites), Pal's structure creates permanence, becoming an eccentric-looking landmark.

It's easy to laugh off the Pal's fast-food pieces—and most programmatic architecture—as campy works of art. They are. Part of the point is to entertain. But it's often also to exalt. While Bristol's "Grand Guitar" building, visible from I-81, sold instruments and housed an AM radio station and a small museum, it also recalled the region's deep music roots as the "Birthplace of Country Music" to cars that blew past. "Overall our reaction to a Programmatic structure is ideological and only incidentally visual," architectural historian David Gebhard has argued.[14] So the lowly hot dog—a cheap and glorious tube of scraps—becomes monument and monumental at Pal's, where it sits atop a teal pedestal of sorts, announcing its import within a specific region. It's sized for a giant. But it's food for the people.

NOTES

1. Emily Hilliard, "Slaw Abiding Citizens: A Quest for the West Virginia Hot Dog," *Gravy* 61 (Fall 2016): 29.

2. Robert Venturi, Denise Scott Brown, and Steven Izenour, *Learning from Las Vegas: The Forgotten Symbolism of Architectural Form*, rev. ed. (Cambridge, MA: MIT Press, 1977).

3. David Gebhard, "Programmatic Architecture: An Introduction," *SCA Journal* 13, no. 2 (Spring–Summer 1995): 2.

4. Giants like the one at Pal's #2 were later dubbed Muffler Men for the car parts they often held and can be traced to a mold from Bob Prewitt's studio in Lawndale, California, originally conceived as ax-wielding Paul Bunyans, and often repurposed to hold and advertise all manner of products. Brian Butko and Sarah Butko, *Roadside Giants* (Mechanicsburg, PA: Stackpole Books, 2005), 15–19.

5. Robin Abcarian, "Standouts—Even in Venice," *Los Angeles Times*, June 16, 1993, http://articles.latimes.com/1993-06-16/news/vw-3738_1_venice-canals.

6. "About the Artists," Karen and Tony Barone, accessed December 11, 2017, https://www.baroneart.com/about-the-artists; Abcarian, "Standouts—Even in Venice."

7. Karen and Tony Barone, phone interview by Emily Wallace, September 25, 2017.

8. Thom Crosby, interview by Emily Wallace, Johnson City, Tennessee, July 20, 2017.

9. Karen and Tony Barone, interview.

10. "Company History," Valleydale, accessed December 11, 2017, https://www.valleydale.com/company/companyhistory.html.

11. Thom Crosby, email to the author, December 11, 2017.

12. Fred Sauceman, interview by *Still Journal*, accessed December 10, 2017, http://www.stilljournal.net/fred-sauceman-interview.php.

13. Crosby, interview.

14. Gebhard, "Programmatic Architecture," 2.

Chapter 10

Confessions of a Spear Packer

Robert Gipe

WHEN I graduated college and first got an interview for a full-time job, I went to the library and found a book on how to write a resume.

It said one should put quantifiable stuff on one's resume. "Sales increased 15% while I was under-assistant marketing director." "I had responsibility for seventeen salespeople working in an eight-county area." That kind of thing.

But I was an English major. I'd never done anything quantifiable.

So I put that I could pack eight hundred and forty jars of pickles in an eight-hour shift.

Which is true. I can. I worked in a pickle factory one summer when I was in college.

What I didn't put on my resume was that the pickle factory where I worked paid you by the hour based on your rate of production over the span of a week.

That meant if one packed as hard as one could all day long all week one got paid ten or twelve dollars an hour.

That was a nice chunk of change in 1986, which was when I worked in the cucumber economy.

We packed spears at my pickle factory, and the spears had to be packed with the seeds all facing out, so that the discriminating pickle shopper could gauge the freshness of the spear.

Factory management couldn't figure out how to get a machine to pack the spears in the jar with the seed sides out, although all summer long they sent engineers to stand and watch us pack. The engineers tried to figure out how to design a machine to replace us. But they couldn't. Not in the summer of '86.

This is the way of the spear line: one had a partner and one had a stainless-steel tray of fresh cucumber spears—our factory packed spears the day the cucumbers were picked. The fresh cucumbers were cut into spears and fed into a hopper of brine. A worker brought a fishnet full of spears and spilled them out into one's tray, and one went to packing.

1. USE TWO-FINGER SPEAR TECHNIQUE.

To pack a jar of spears, one puts two fingers against the skin side of a spear and then lines the inside of the jar with spears—seed out, seed out, seed out—so they were standing against the inside of the jar. Then one took a handful of spears and shoved them in the middle with a pop of the flat of one's hand. Then one put the jar upside down on a shelf above one's tray and a checker came and punched one's card every time one got a case of twelve jars. The checkers checked the jars to make sure all the spears were seed out. They shook the jars to make sure they were packed tight. If the spears came out, one had to redo that jar. But once one got the hang of it, one didn't have to repack much.

2. LINE JAR WITH SPEARS. SEEDS OUT!

It should be said one is supposed to wear latex gloves while packing. It should be said most packers can't pack as fast wearing latex gloves.

3. TAKE HANDFULL OF SPEARS.

One day I was packing without my gloves, and I had a hang-nail long as a fish hook, and I was tearing it open every time my hand went over the edge of the jar. So I put a Band-Aid over the hangnail.

4. JAM SPEARS IN CENTER OF JAR.

I was rolling along, hangnail and all—seed out, seed out, seed out, middle handful pop; seed out, seed out, seed out, middle hand-ful pop—and I looked up and my Band-Aid wasn't on my finger. I looked around for it in my tray and it wasn't there. I looked on the floor for it and it wasn't there. It became clear there was only one place it could've gone.

In a jar.

They hated to stop that spear line, boy, they hated to stop that line.

But I called my checker over, and said, "Buddy, I think I sent a Band-Aid through the line," and the checker said, "It don't matter, they pasteurize them after they get to y'all."

I was comforted enough by this information to go back to work, although I still thought from time to time that summer of that Band-Aid, perhaps concealed in the center of the jar, so that no one ever noticed, and the jar shipped and stocked and bought and opened—perhaps at a cookout, where a mother, and then a whole family, and then the whole picnic ground recoiled in horror at the sight of my Band-Aid, all of them running through the picnic area waving their arms and screaming. I imagined lawyers engaged and the whole company going down in a hail of bad publicity over my pickled Band-Aid, all the spear packers and cucumber farmers thrown out of work.

5. SMACK JAR.

6. SHAKE JAR UPSIDE DOWN.

7. REPEAT.

In time though, I put my worries aside. I got the job I applied for with the pickle statistics on my resume (I told the story of the Band-Aid in my interview!) and mostly forgot about the pickle factory.

I had a chance in later life to ask about the spear line, and was told the factory was still there, but they shut down the spear line, and no longer hired an army of spear packers every summer. The person I asked said people don't care anymore if their spears aren't seed side out.

What does it mean for that work to go out of the world? That company had all us working just so their pickles would look better on the shelf. Fearless in their freshness. Quietly saying to the discriminating pickle shopper, we welcome your scrutiny.

There is risk in presenting oneself as human, capable of pride, capable of failure. There is risk in doing things in labor-intensive ways. More spear packers means more Band-Aids, more potential for disaster. More expense. The savvy pickle company owner knows they are better off without them. If no one packs seed side out, then what difference does it make?

One might say, "I buy my pickles at the farmers market." Or "My friends make pickles and my Frigidaire is full of delicious artisanal pickles." One might make a point about scale, knowing one's pickle packer, about brining local.

I loved the spear line. I loved the sight of all of us down the row of stainless-steel trays going as hard as we could go in our hairnets and our plastic aprons and our ungloved hands. I loved all of us lounging around outside the plant during break, buying hot dogs from a food truck, arguing with the farmers about who had it rougher. I loved when the line stopped and the most ambitious packers scurried for jars while the rest of us smoked and complained. All that is gone, and I have no idea what English majors quantify on their resumes.

I wish it were easier to count. I wish it was easier for things to count, for people to count. I wish I'd worn my gloves. I'm sorry.

Chapter 11

"Good Luck in Preserving": Canning and the Uncanny in Appalachia

Danille Elise Christensen

> So you're going to can and freeze. . . . Yours will be
> a fine sense of accomplishment when you review
> the rows of healthful, colorful jars of fruits, meats
> and vegetables on your shelves and in your freezer.
> . . . This book is planned to give you simple, easy-to-
> follow directions, to tell you everything you need to
> know about these processes. Good Luck!
>
> *(Atlas Book of Recipes,* 1952)[1]

IN 2015, driving home to Ohio after house hunting in southwest Virginia, I pulled off for a bite at the Korean restaurant halfway between
Blacksburg and the West Virginia border. It was closed—only open
for lunch on the weekend—but as I wandered through the antiques
shop next door I saw a square-shouldered fruit jar, badly etched,

and stained with rust where a wire had once fastened a glass cap. I'd grown up canning and was researching the practice in the United States, so I owned plenty of jars already. Still, the bottle caught my eye: rather than bearing a brand signature or company emblem, its cloudy face was dominated by an embossed heart-leaved four-leaf clover, veined and stemmed. "ATLAS," the jar proclaimed in raised letters. "GOOD-LUCK." It felt like a sign, this battered but optimistic vessel. I gave the shop clerk a couple of bucks and took it home to clean it.

A few months later, I encountered the Good Luck jar again, this time in a photograph (Figure 11.1).[2] Two girls wearing headbands emblazoned with the 4-H Club clover hold prizewinning string beans up for the camera. Their jars, like mine, are square, with rounded corners and "Lightning-finish" tops: unlike Mason jars, whose threaded necks were patented by John Landis Mason in 1858, these have glass lids attached to a smooth neck by a pivoting wire bail.[3] And one jar clearly bears the outline of a four-leaf clover.

11.1. United States Department of Agriculture, "Two Prize Winners with Their String Beans," c. 1920s. From *When We're Green We Grow* by Jane S. McKimmon, illustration facing page 111. Copyright © 1945 by the University of North Carolina Press. Used by permission of the publisher. www.uncpress.org.

The photo must have been snapped sometime after 1920, when the Hazel-Atlas Glass Company—headquartered in Wheeling, West Virginia—started making its Good Luck jars. Company correspondence from August 1921 reveals that this new embossed line catered to a special population: "the trade which prefers square jars." Retaining a standard-size opening and compatible with standard rubber rings, the jar was functionally identical to other vessels on the market. But aesthetically, and in keeping with marketing trends that emphasized consumer psychology, it targeted "artistic" canners who "desire[d] a more unique . . . container." The jar's "crystal flint glass" and "neatly designed trade-mark" made it "especially attractive for exhibit purposes and for home canned products put up for sale." Throughout the 1920s, Hazel-Atlas promoted the jars for "fancy packs or exhibit purposes," an upscale, modern alternative to the Atlas E-Z Seal Round Jar. In short, clover-bedecked Good Luck jars were meant for those who made canning public, who displayed care, skill, and creativity in social spaces like competitions, markets, and gift exchanges.[4]

The two 4-H girls were engaged in just this kind of public performance. Their photo appears in *When We're Green We Grow*, Jane S. McKimmon's 1945 history of USDA home demonstration education in North Carolina. In 1913, at the beginning of her pioneering agricultural extension work with girls and women, McKimmon chose a "square, clear glass jar" to be used by canning club participants in fifteen southern states. The young women planned, raised, preserved, and sold their own products, keeping the profits for themselves. Although most early club efforts—primarily tomatoes— were packed and sold in metal cans, organizers recognized the marketing potential of colorless, transparent ("flint") glass. During the first exhibition of North Carolina girls' canning club work, the groups were allotted a corner of the machinery building at the 1913 State Fair in Raleigh. There, the "uniform clear glass jars with their colorful contents"—peaches, figs, berries, string beans, and a vegetable soup mixture—"made an attractive oasis in that desert of iron and steel"; further, they generated robust business.[5]

Here, then, is a curious domestic object. Intended for public display, allied with commerce, the Good Luck jar was turned to these ends not by businessmen, but by women and girls. That is, the jar and its contexts of use begin to tell a story about gender. But follow other features of this artifact—the glass it's made from, the lightning-style closure, the question of "good luck," the embossed clover— and new insights emerge. What follows is a tale of innovation and labor, self-representation and misrepresentation, the blurring of regional boundaries, and the communication of local values. It is not a tidy story, but that should not surprise us.

GAS-FIRED GLASS: "OF THE MOST MODERN AND PRACTICAL TYPE"

> "The bottle industry . . . has done and will continue to do much toward advancement of the State of West Virginia."
>
> ("The Bottle Industry," 1929)[6]

I grew up in Columbus, Ohio, at the confluence of the Scioto and Olentangy Rivers and various tributaries that cut their paths through oily shale and fossil-filled limestone. We were edged by the Allegheny Plateau, a space I knew as a haven of sandy caves and shady hollows. My parents moved there, to Appalachian Ohio, after I graduated from high school, but the hills had long been the destination of school trips and family wanderings. An elementary teacher born in southeastern Ohio took us creeking, pointing out shagbark and hemlock, salamanders and crawdads. Underneath them, he said, lay clay and also gas, the kind that burned with a blue flame.

The deep fields of compressed sediment that link New York to Indiana have shaped the material culture of the humans who live above them—which is why containers of clay and glass figure alongside trees and stone in my mental map of eastern Ohio.

Driving to summer camp, we counted the pottery billboards near
Zanesville, a historic home of utilitarian stoneware. Setting out for
a picnic at Hocking Hills State Park, an hour south of Columbus, we
passed the Anchor Hocking building in Lancaster, once the world's
largest producer of glass tableware. Its factories, like those up north
along Lake Erie, were fueled by cheap natural gas that could push
furnaces to 2,600 degrees Fahrenheit. And across the Ohio River
lay West Virginia—whose own reserves of silica and hydrocarbons
made the glass industry the state's fourth-largest employer by
1910. In the early decades of the twentieth century, members of the
American Flint Glass Workers' Union moved back and forth across
state lines, and up and down the Ohio River, finding work at factories in Ohio, Pennsylvania, West Virginia, Indiana, and Kentucky,
where they lived in politically progressive "glass towns."[7]

Though Appalachia is often imagined as entirely rural and
beholden to coal, the Good Luck jar reminds us of alternate visions
and economic trajectories. Narratives of Appalachia as a productive,
innovative space are highlighted by today's Museum of American
Glass in West Virginia (located in Weston), but they were promoted
by twentieth-century regional periodicals as well. In a 1928 article
enumerating all the "West Virginia Manufactured Articles That
May Be Used in the Home," Mrs. Phil [Pearl Scott] Conley noted that
the state was the nation's second-largest producer of glassware and
pottery. The next year her husband catalogued a department store
window display prepared for the 1929 gubernatorial inauguration;
included among its "Made in West Virginia" offerings were wool
blankets, a brass firehose nozzle, a telephone, and glass items from
eight different manufacturers.[8] At least one glassmaking company
with extensive West Virginia connections was not represented in
the inaugural exhibit: Hazel-Atlas, whose workers produced the jar
I bought in Pembroke, Virginia.

By 1929, Hazel-Atlas had been a fixture in Wheeling for at least
thirty years, so its absence from the exhibit is curious. The company's precursor, Hazel Glass, began in Wellsburg, West Virginia, a
city on the Ohio River that had been manufacturing glass since 1813.

After the patent for John Mason's threaded-neck (or in collectors' terms, "Mason-finish") jar expired in 1879, enterprises like Ball Brothers Glass Company flooded the glass fruit jar market. In fall 1885, Hazel Glass founders Charles Brady and Charles Tallman entered the fray by building relationships with a number of local enterprises. Their first product was an opal ("milk") glass disk meant to top the mouth-blown fruit jars of the Bellaire Stamping Company, located about twenty-five miles downriver. Hazel's white glass inserts were held in place by a metal screw band and made from molten glass produced in Wellsburg's own Riverside Glass works—of which Charles Brady happened to be president. According to one admirer, Riverside had "initiated the exclusive use of natural gas in the manufacture of glassware," and Brady became known as an innovator.[9]

As the nineteenth century closed, Hazel Glass produced a range of home canning products, including an opaque glass disk immerser (which kept fruit submerged in syrup) and a safety-valve jar (which had a glass top held in place by a spring clamp). Charles Brady's brothers started their own businesses, making fruit jars, zinc caps, and jelly tumblers. By 1902, the Bradys had consolidated their jar and closure ventures, and the Hazel-Atlas Glass Company was born. Holdings included a manufacturing plant built in Wheeling, West Virginia, in 1898, and one constructed in Clarksburg two years later.[10]

The men in charge always emphasized forward thinking. "Everything about the several plants of the Hazel-Atlas Glass Company," wrote one assessor in 1910, "is of the most modern and practical type, old machinery being promptly relegated to the junk heap with each new discovery or improvement in the methods of manufacture." Hazel-Atlas chairman J.C. Brady began a 1929 article in *West Virginia Review* with the folksy tagline "Tall Oaks from Little Acorns Grow," but his retrospective emphasizes engineering expertise and maximum efficiency through automation.[11]

The Brady brothers intended from the first to "supplant and displace hand work" in an attempt to make "glass containers cheaper than tin cans." In the nineteenth century, Hazel Glass had used a Merry-Go-Round press that rotated glass molds around the edge of a table, while its linked company, Atlas, made the first fruit jars fabricated by "machine methods," using a semiautomatic contraption designed and patented in 1894 by Charles E. Blue, a Wheeling native. In September 1896, Atlas was turning out 30,000 green glass Mason jars a day, while Hazel used the same machine to make more expensive flint glass jars. Advertising underscored that these were no handmade containers: a 1906 brochure praises Hazel-Atlas jars as strong and even, with smooth screw threads unlikely to break when consumers applied metal caps and rubber gaskets.[12]

In the teens, Hazel-Atlas glass plants in Clarksburg and in Washington, Pennsylvania, were kept humming because the company had gained access to the new Owens machine in May 1909. Six years earlier, Point Pleasant native Michael Joseph Owens, a glassblower for J. H. Hobbs, Brockunier and Company in Wheeling, had revolutionized glassmaking when he invented a rotating device that used vacuum pressure to pull molten glass into molds. The fully automated Owens machine created bottles of consistent weight and uniform thickness and potentiated new shapes, such as the "rounded square" so favored by Jane McKimmon and her 4-H charges.[13]

Over its lifetime, Hazel-Atlas produced seventy-three different jars, including the Strong Shoulder threaded Mason and the Atlas E-Z Seal, a widemouthed jar trademarked in 1911 and billed as "the first complete machine-made glass top Lightning Seal style." The latter ushered in a "new era" for "the housekeeper," offering her "smooth perfect fitting" rims and covers that were devoid of glass dust and corrosive metals and, of course, were "E-Z to operate." Promotional materials championed the machine-made jar's "durability and efficiency for home canning." Clearly, the Bradys were invested in both the narrative and the material production of modernity. These Hazel-Atlas wares and documents were distributed nationally but had an especially strong presence in the Mid-Atlantic, the upland South, and the Midwest manufacturing corridors.[14]

Regional connections are reflected in a 1924 Hazel-Atlas cookbook printed in Wheeling. The booklet highlights rural practices like seed saving and hog butchering, noting that glass jars are useful for protecting seeds from insects and mice and will keep lard "fresh and sweet for years." It offers recipes for pressure-canned brains, as well as hogshead cheese (souse). Sausage patties meant to be preserved, the cookbook advises, should be partially fried and packed in gravy or their own drippings; the book's writers compare their recipes for canned bulk sausage to similar products histori- cally prepared in open jars, crocks, or buckets. Other foodways that have come to be associated with Appalachia also receive notice: here are recipes for pressure-canned rabbit and squirrel, instruc- tions for making lye hominy, a suggestion that canning sauerkraut will keep it crisp. Across the back cover, bottle-bodied imps with a single corkscrew curl parade fruits, vegetables, and meats while a Good Luck jar hovers overhead (Figure 11.2).[15]

11.2. Back cover (detail) of *A Book of Recipes and Helpful Information on Canning*, 4th ed. (Wheeling, WV: Hazel-Atlas Glass Co., 1924).

The story of a progressive state and region linked to the rest of the nation by robust production and commerce has been largely superseded by other tales, narratives that trail a clandestine magic, like the imps on the Hazel-Atlas manual. One example: Upturning a glass jar often reveals a number on the base that names the position of the jar's mold in a glassmaking machine. The numeral 13 is rare because most machines had no more than ten positions, and new numbers were added only when a mold broke and had to be replaced. But antique dealers sometimes sell canning jars marked with "13" for a higher price, telling potential buyers that they're hard to find because moonshiners broke thirteeners to avoid bad luck.[16] A related representation: until recently, canning jars were featured at the History Museum of Western Virginia in Roanoke, where whiskey joined coal in the permanent "regional industries" display. Crates of Mason-finish jars abutted an old copper turnip-top still; in illuminated kiosks, Ball jars filled with amber liquid captured the light, invoking the warmth of corn liquor. Although a photo elsewhere in the exhibit revealed that home distillers have used white plastic milk jugs for decades, in this installation fruit jars were tasked with telling the story of illegal bootlegging. In other settings—and despite its automated, industrial origins—the home canning jar continues to elicit notions of illicit, superstitious lifeways. After all, it's just a small step from Lightning closures to white lightning.

LUCK AND CORN LIKKER: APPALACHIA, UNCANNY

It is lightning, in fact, that sets the stage for one typically stereotypical depiction of the region as backwoods nightmare—canning jars included. A 1996 episode of sci-fi drama *The X-Files* opens as lightning cracks outside a decrepit antebellum farmhouse, illuminating a scythe resting near junked cars and a severed pig's head lolling on the steps of a deep porch. Inside, the Peacock boys—physically deformed and mentally deficient—act on instinct and feel no pain. As we watch them gathered around the meal table, they cut an umbilical cord with bloodied scissors, then bury a tiny malformed body in a shallow, muddy hole. The horrors of the episode—titled simply "Home"—begin in a kitchen, filthy and dark, where unwashed enameled pans teeter alongside feeble oil lamps and obsolete zinc-topped Mason jars. The meat-like contents of these old-timey vessels are as repellent as the toothless, inbred relics who put them up, who butcher their own hogs and booby-trap the house against outsiders.[17]

Set in Home, Pennsylvania, an unincorporated village in northern Appalachia, the episode is classic eighteenth-century Gothic, all exaggerated marvels and frights, life-threatening monsters and madmen. But other details invoke the uncanny—what Freud called the *Unheimlich*, the estranged familiar. This is a more uneasy sort of terror, eerie, generated by the surfacing of something half-recognized that disrupts definitions and refuses to let us wholly dis-identify and disengage. In the nineteenth century, writes Brian McCuskey, live-in servants troubled the clear binaries around which bourgeois life was structured: cooks, maids, and nannies were intimate strangers who transgressed public/private boundaries and upturned class, gender, and race hierarchies as they taught and served their masters' children. Consequently, in popular literature the attics, basements, and kitchens in which these servants lived and worked were depicted as threatening, spooky spaces.[18] Thus, the Peacocks' kitchen in Home/"Home"—and the food and people produced therein—are more than menacing and dirty: they too are Unheimlich, uncanny. Viewers layer onto this fetid vision of domesticity other, more familiar and intimate, scenes: neighbors finding warmth in rendering lard and shared labor during frosty hog-killings; women gathering to process peaches and crabapple jelly, imbuing the jeweled jars with starry cloves and cinnamon candies, family secrets.

It seems strange to think of canning as uncanny. Yet the Good Luck jar reminds us that risk and even death have long been associated with this home-based process. For decades, people didn't know why some jars soured and the contents of others killed whole families. *Clostridium botulinum* is a curious organism whose spores create toxins only in hospitable environments—but those optimal conditions depend on a range of complex interacting factors, including levels of oxygen, moisture, acid, salt, sugar, humidity, and heat; the density of the product; the length of time it's heated; and the presence of competing organisms.[19] Even as the home canning industry promoted this kind of food preservation as critical to family success, companies underscored the mysterious or uncertain aspects of the craft. They wished customers "Good Luck" in their instruction manuals and incised the phrase on jar molds. Before World War II, popular Good Luck rubber rings were branded with the ancient auspicious symbol variously known as *manji*, fylfot, or *sauwastika* (Figures 11.3A and 11.3B). (Due to Nazi transformation of this figure as the *Hakenkreuz*, contemporary viewers may see menace in promotional materials intended to invoke domestic harmony and good fortune.)

But it's not just canning jars that mark the kitchen in "Home" as dangerous—it's the fact that *X-files* fans encounter the space as an embodiment of Appalachia. Time and again in popular discourse, the region rises as the living dead: horror films and tourism brochures alike paint landscape and people as unlikely and impoverished survivals of the past in the present. In these representations, the mountains are dramatically othered, or else paternalistically familiared, as places that follow their own logics—where local knowledges (coded as "superstition") can be deadly or merely ineffectual, but always antithetical to progress.[20] One compendium of Kentucky beliefs published by Princeton University Press in 1920 asserted that "mountain whites" and "lowland negroes" were more likely than "lowland whites" to confuse coincidence with cause. More dangerously, under the guise of sustenance and safety, servants from these populations ostensibly passed superstitions along to the white wealthier children in their care, introducing "terror, doubt, and division" to otherwise comfortable domestic life.[21]

In the national imagination, Appalachians have played the roles of both servant and child, laboring for absent bosses and

11.3A and 3B. This pamphlet for Good Luck Rubbers (rubber jar rings) incorporates the ancient auspicious symbol variously known as *manji*, fylfot, or *sauwastika*. Back and front covers, *Good Luck in Preserving*, 3d ed. (East Cambridge, MA: Boston Woven Hose & Rubber Co., c. 1917), courtesy The Minnetrista Heritage Center, Muncie, Indiana.

subject to regimes of improvement and enlightenment. An evangelistic magazine called *World Outlook* emphasized both identities in November 1919, linking them to magic and mountains in the process. The cover featured a weathered man in suspenders gazing away from a log home, prepping readers for the photoessay inside: "A Race of Rip Van Winkles Is Waking Up." Published by the Methodist Episcopal Church's Board of Home Missions, the story aimed to introduce readers to "our southern highlanders": "the most interesting, most hospitable, and in some instances, the most needy folk" in the country. Subheadings included "Living at a Standstill" and "Raising Babies By Luck." Excerpts from the piece were republished in the next year's *Literary Digest*, under the title "The Southern Highlanders Wake Up, but Still Make Corn 'Likker.'"[22]

These are enduring images in popular discourse: moonshine in flint glass fruit jars; static communities sleepwalking through domestic life, leaving their fates to chance; genetically degraded maniacs still using zinc caps in 1996. They contrast sharply with the production of modernity so carefully cultivated by Appalachian industrialists—including the makers of Hazel-Atlas Good Luck jars.

My experience suggests that popular representations may also misread how *luck* can function in mountain communities. In recorded interviews Appalachian interlocutors do use the word, but rarely in reference to supernatural belief or procedural insecurity. Instead, to admit that one has had "good luck" is to simultaneously signal and deflect recognition of superior work. Carrie Severt, recorded in Ennice, North Carolina, in autumn 1978, loved hominy, even though making it with lye from wood ashes was "a long hard job." After describing exactly how it was done, she remarked, "I used to have good luck with hominy, but I ain't made none in a year or two." Arlene Chaney, of Estill County, Kentucky, observed in 2012 that her natal family had "the worst luck" with gardening, then placed this seemingly random outcome in perspective, laughing that maybe her family had "more other things that we thought was more important than a garden." She made a "crispy and good" fourteen-day pickle, but didn't have "any luck" with lime pickles, which were the specialty of others in the community. She acknowledged the reputation of her yeast rolls, a success due to efficient planning, use of fresh yeast, and strategic refrigeration, but concluded, "I just always had good luck with em I guess"—and goes on to mention a failure with bread raised from a friend's starter.

As these women invoke luck, I hear them positioning success amid apparent or possible failures, thereby mitigating elevation of self and masking disparagement of others (Figure 11.4). Underneath this humble talk is recognition that skill and experience matter more than the ineffable assistance of an incantation or a magic imp. Said Chaney, with a laugh, "My mom used to tell me, well, she didn't see but one thing wrong with my cooking: I wouldn't cook enough."[23]

CANNED PEACHES
HAZEL BURKEY, Greeneville, Tenn.
TOMATO PICKLES
MAY MATHERLY, Harrodsburg, Ky.

CANNED TOMATOES
SALLIE LISTER, Greeneville, Tenn.
CANNED CORN
MATTIE CONER, Killen, Ala.

11.4. Hazel Burkey and Sallie Lister, both from Greeneville, Tennessee, produced canned peaches and tomatoes that were featured in *A Book of Recipes and Helpful Information on Canning*, 4th ed. (Wheeling, WV: Hazel-Atlas Glass Co., 1924), alongside green tomato pickles from central Kentucky and canned corn put up in Appalachian Alabama.

IN CLOVER: HEAD HAND HEART HEALTH

Not all the Good Luck jars feature a clover—the half-pint versions don't have enough surface area. But this small leaf is worth investigating more closely. Doing so sheds light on the calibration of practice to values, the relationships between careful mastery and "luck," and the ways mountain people and institutions have participated in broader movements and goals.

Clover, after all, is ubiquitous, global. Hundreds of species do what clover does best: provide fodder for foraging mammals, nectar for pollinators, nitrogen for future growing things. Indigenous peoples in North America used clover for food and for medicine—in poultices for burns and in syrups for bronchial troubles. It's no wonder that the prosperous are said to be "rolling in clover," or that for centuries Europeans have linked rare four-leaved specimens to wealth, matrimony, and enhanced power. Possessing a four-leaf clover, one might see fairies and break enchantments. Among Kentucky mountaineers, ordinary clover—boiled in a kettle, with mineral rock—made a good skin salve, but leaves with four lobes affected the heart: to find true love, said the knowing in the 1920s, hold one aloft and make a wish, or swallow it whole.[24]

The iconic four-leaved emblem of 4-H actually began its life in Iowa—with three leaves. In the first decade of the twentieth century, when Page County students developed a symbol for their fledgling after-school country-life clubs, they were more interested in the plant's practical morality than in magic. The three-leaved clover pin—designed with a kernel of corn in the center and the word "Iowa" on the stem—was meant to honor students at school Junior Achievement Shows. It showcased the related domains of technology, agriculture, and domestic science and the bodily involvement of head, heart, and hands. By 1912, "home" had been added to the mix, and the Page County Boys' and Girls' 3-H clubs had become 4-H clubs. That was the year the boys' corn-judging team won the state competition for the third consecutive year. But chalk the victory up to skill, not luck: the previous year, their

teacher and guide Jessie Field had enrolled in a corn-judging class—
the lone woman among two hundred male students—and took
home a prize for doing the best work.[25]

People from all over the country—educators and adminis-
trators—had visited Superintendent Field's Page County schools,
and home demonstration agents in the southern states formally
adopted the clover insignia in 1913. When canning club girls began
marketing their goods commercially, their labels bore a four-leaved
clover. "The 4-H brand represents Head, Hand, Heart, and Health,"
wrote Jane McKimmon in her history of US Department of Agriculture clubwork in North Carolina. "In the production of a product
which shall rank with the best standards, the *Head* is developed by
devising ways and means, and evolving plans. The *Hand* is taught
to cunningly and systematically execute. The *Heart* grows big
enough to take in all other workers and bids the hand lend assistance wherever it is needed. The *Health* is promoted by wholesome
work in the fresh air and the happy commingling of friends and
neighbors."[26] The four-leaved logo came into general use when the
boys' and girls' clubs were incorporated into national USDA Extension Program work in 1914.

The clover on the Hazel-Atlas Good Luck jar targeted the
women and girls engaged in this four-pronged endeavor. It appealed
to their sense of branding, actively encouraging "exhibit purposes"
for those who had planned, executed, supported, and informed
each other in the course of bottling the foods they'd raised to sell.
Simultaneously, however, the design overlaid these public and economically productive female endeavors with a bit of magic and an
undercurrent of uncertainty: good luck?

Further, the conditions of production that created these jars
were out of step with 4-H goals; handcraftsmanship and happy
commingling had little place in the modern glassworks. For every
Owens machine brought into the Hazel-Atlas plant, writes historian Joan Weiskircher, five workers—four of them highly skilled
and well paid—lost their jobs. One 1929 booster couched such losses
in the name of progress, praising automation for reducing child

labor and raising the standard of living for more employees, since an artisan glass blower no longer "received the lion's share in salary while the employees performing other duties received very little for their labors."[27] This egalitarian ethos was belied by the realities of gender and race within the company. Most employees at the Hazel-Atlas cap-making plant in Wheeling, for instance, were women, who did dirty and tedious jobs feeding tin and packing products; all were unmarried until World War II, and all were white until the mid-1950s, when desegregation laws mandated consideration of black applicants. At company headquarters in Wheeling—a four-story brick and sandstone art deco showpiece with a three-story glass entrance portal—women earned low wages but got discounts on dinnerware. The janitress, the sole black worker in the building, used a separate restroom in the utility room.[28]

Cooperation and exploitation, camaraderie and fear, reason and magic, skill and danger, the Familiar and the Other—all may be called up by my clover-embossed Hazel-Atlas Good Luck jar, at once squarely solid (Atlas bore the weight of heaven) and gracefully fanciful (those four-part leaves, that gently curved stem). Head, hand, heart, health. Botulism and backwardness, decay and death. "Good Luck in Preserving."

ANECDOTES OF THE JAR

In 1918, just a few years before Hazel-Atlas started making the Good Luck jar, insurance company executive Wallace Stevens was in Elizabethton, Tennessee, doing business with lumber companies cutting old-growth forest in that northeastern corner of the state. Stevens was also a modernist poet, and during his time in Elizabethton he wrote his own story of glass in Appalachia.

> I placed a jar in Tennessee,
> And round it was, upon a hill.
> It made the slovenly wilderness
> Surround that hill.

The wilderness rose up to it,
And sprawled around, no longer wild.
The jar was round upon the ground
And tall and of a port in air.

It took dominion everywhere.
The jar was gray and bare.
It did not give of bird or bush,
Like nothing else in Tennessee.

Stevens's poem is titled, simply, "Anecdote of the Jar." Some critics read it as a rejection of romanticism, a musing on the ready-made or "the perfection of empty form," a meditation on perspective and power and the imposition of human will. It must be a moonshine (i.e., a Mason) jar, they suggest, an empty bottle of white lightning out there in the ramshackle wilds of Appalachia. And perhaps, as East Tennessee State University professor Kevin O'Donnell has suggested, "Anecdote of the Jar" reflects on the environmental impact of local resource extraction in the service of national and international markets.[29]

For me, the piece embodies the contrasts of Hazel-Atlas's Good Luck jar. Aligned with science in both manufacture and use, these bottles were emblazoned with emblems of superstition. A product of self-consciously modern mass production, they offered a colorful respite from industrial ugliness and were filled with locally rooted and resonant food. Used for decades in print and visual media to index a regional backwardness just strange enough to be dangerous, at one time the jars also enabled women and girls to enter mainstream markets and display skill and creativity in public forums.

"Anecdote of the Jar" came to mind in 2016 as I traveled not through the hills of Tennessee, but across those of southeastern Ohio. Lured by cases of Ball jars in the plate glass window, I stopped at Midwest Glassware Outlet in Hocking County. Ball had recently rolled out an Elite series, including miniature jars that couldn't be hermetically sealed, spiral-shaped vessels easy to drink from, hexagonal "sharing" jars for putting up artisanal gifts, and plain unembossed bottles perfect for the minimalist. The Ball brand, I knew, was now licensed to Jarden, a Ball Corporation spin-off that also produced Kerr jars. Cases of both had filled the storeroom of our house in Columbus and later ringed my parents' garage down in the hills, near Athens. Some bottles marked with Hazel-Atlas's "H over A" stood on our shelves, too, migrating there as gifts from neighbors and in-laws and grandparents, but they were rare surprises: Hazel-Atlas jars haven't been produced since the mid-1960s.[30]

I left the outlet in Logan an hour later, having purchased a few of the new "elite" jars for research purposes. As I entered the sky-blue metal-trussed bridge that crosses the Ohio River near Ravenswood, West Virginia, I thought of the vessels waiting for me at home in Blacksburg: a stoneware mug hand-painted with the leaves and fruit of *Aesculus glabra*, the Ohio buckeye; bright orange midcentury opaque glass cereal bowls made in Columbus by Federal Glass (early associated with Hazel-Atlas's Charles N. Brady); a clover-embossed bottle holding dishmops under my kitchen sink.[31] And I could see that jar set on a mountainside in Tennessee, modern in form and manufacture, unyielding in material, surveilling the woods that rise around it, its production fueled by ancient forests that lie beneath. A glassy, alien port; a bottle thoroughly domestic and cheerfully mundane. Uncanny.

NOTES

1. *Atlas Book of Recipes and Helpful Information on Home Canning and Freezing* (Wheeling, WV: Hazel-Atlas Glass Company, 1952), 3. Folder 18, M/M John J. Pruis Collection (2000.71.13), The Minnetrista Heritage Center, Muncie, Indiana.

2. Just as some Hazel-Atlas jars were made with molds marked "E-Z Seal" and others were produced using molds marked "EZ Seal," my Good Luck jar has a hyphen, while some otherwise similar jars do not. Company literature and collectors' guides reference the jars using the unhyphenated form.

3. The distinctive "lightning" closure, which seals with the aid of a separate rubber ring, was invented by Henry William Putnam. As a young man he sold drinking water to forty-niners during the California gold rush; later he patented a reusable wire fastener that held

bottle corks in place. In the 1870s, Putnam and two other men, Charles de Quillfeldt and Karl Hutter, secured a patent on easy-open (lightning-quick) "swing stoppers" for beer and champagne bottles; in 1882, Putnam patented a similar closure for bottles with wider mouths. The Lightning fruit jar became "the only meaningful long-term competitor with the Mason screw lid"; Bill Lockhart, Beau Schriever, Bill Lindsey, and Carol Serr, "Henry W. Putnam and the Lightning Fastener," in *Encyclopedia of Manufacturer's Marks on Glass Containers*, comp. and ed. Bottle Research Group, Volume H–I, Society for Historical Archaeology, Historic Glass Bottle Identification & Information Website, March 23, 2016, https://sha.org/bottle/pdffiles/HenryPutnam.pdf.

    4. Julian Harrison Toulouse, *Fruit Jars* (Nashville: Nelson, [1969] 1977); Dick Roller, *The Standard Fruit Jar Reference* (Paris, IL: Acorn Press, 1983), 17; Roland Marchand, *Advertising the American Dream: Making Way for Modernity, 1920–1940* (Berkeley: University of California Press, 1985); Hazel-Atlas Glass Company, *A Book of Recipes and Helpful Information on Canning*, 4th ed. (Wheeling, WV: Hazel-Atlas Glass Co., 1924), 5; Hazel-Atlas Glass Company, *A Book of Recipes and Helpful Information on Canning* (Wheeling, WV: Hazel-Atlas Glass Co., 1926), 6.

    5. Jane Simpson McKimmon, *When We're Green We Grow* (Chapel Hill: University of North Carolina Press, 1945), 109–11. Hazel-Atlas Good Luck jars were discontinued during World War II due to "industrial priority limitations," though a few more were made before 1950 (Roller, *Standard Fruit Jar Reference*, 1983). For more on the value of literal transparency, see Anna Zeide, *Canned: The Rise and Fall of Consumer Confidence in the American Food Industry* (Oakland: University of California Press, 2018); on girls' tomato clubs, see Elizabeth S. D. Engelhardt, *A Mess of Greens: Southern Gender and Southern Food* (Athens: University of Georgia Press, 2011).

    6. "The Bottle Industry in West Virginia," *West Virginia Review*, March 1929, 193.

    7. Brian Alexander, "The Ghost Bosses: The Disintegration of an American Town," *The Atlantic*, March 13, 2017, https://www.theatlantic.com/business/archive/2017/03/lancaster-ohio-glass-house/519351/; "The Bottle Industry," 193; Ken Fones-Wolf, "Glass Industry," *e-WV: The West Virginia Encyclopedia*, August 7, 2012; Ken Fones-Wolf, *Glass Towns: Industry, Labor, and Political Economy in Appalachia, 1890–1930s* (Urbana: University of Illinois Press, 2007).

    8. Mrs. Phil [Pearl Scott] Conley, "West Virginia Manufactured Articles That May Be Used in the Home," *West Virginia Review*, December 1928; Phil Conley, "'Made in West Virginia' Exhibit," *West Virginia Review*, April 1929.

Danille Elise Christensen

9. Ruby A. Greathouse, "Wellsburg," *e-WV: The West Virginia Encyclopedia*, January 23, 2013, https://www.wvencyclopedia.org/articles/983. The Ball brothers, who had originally made wood-jacketed tin paint and kerosene cans in Buffalo, New York, incorporated the Ball Brothers Glass Company in 1886 and branded Mason jars with their name. A few years later the operation moved to Muncie, Indiana, to take advantage of that state's natural gas boom; Earl L. Conn, *Beneficence: Stories about the Ball Families of Muncie* (Muncie, IN: Minnetrista Cultural Foundation, 2003). Bill Lockhart et al., "Hazel-Atlas Glass Co.," *Encyclopedia of Manufacturer's Marks on Glass Containers*, comp. and ed. Bottle Research Group, vol. H–I, Society for Historical Archaeology, Historic Glass Bottle Identification & Information Website, February 16, 2016, https://sha.org/bottle/pdffiles/Hazel-Atlas.pdf; Joseph F. McFarland, "Brady, Charles N.," in *20th Century History of the City of Washington and Washington County, Pennsylvania and Representative Citizens* (Chicago: Richmond-Arnold Publishing, 1910), 1186–87, http://www.pa-roots.org/data/read.php?811,445270.

10. In 1886, after natural gas in Wellsburg started running low, Hazel manufacturing moved to Washington, Pennsylvania, where the factory produced flint glass jars as well as glass oil cans, molasses cans, lamps, and ointment pots; later, Charles Brady started the Atlas Glass Company in order to make fruit jars. In 1899 Joseph C. (J.C.) Brady, Charles's brother and a former officer of the Wheeling Hinge Company, formed Wheeling Metal Co., which made zinc caps for Mason jars. The next year, younger brother William Sobieski (W.S.) Brady (b. 1853) opened Republic Glass Co. in Clarksburg, West Virginia; among other glass articles, his company produced machine-pressed jelly tumblers with polished rims that could be reused as drinking tumblers. See J. C. Brady, "Hazel-Atlas Glass Company," *West Virginia Review*, March 1929, 189; Lockhart et al., "Hazel-Atlas"; Joan Weiskircher, "Hazel-Atlas: A Home-Grown Corporation," *West Virginia Historical Society Quarterly* 17, no. 2 (April 2003), http://www.wvculture.org/history/wvhs/wvhs1721.html.

11. McFarland, "Brady, Charles N.," 1187; Brady, "Hazel-Atlas Glass," 189.

12. Brady, "Hazel-Atlas Glass," 189; Lockhart et al., "Hazel-Atlas"; Roller, *Standard Fruit Jar Reference.*

13. Lockhart et al., "Hazel-Atlas"; "The Bottle Industry"; Weiskircher, "Hazel-Atlas"; Michael J. Owens, "Glass-Shaping Machine," United States Patent US766768A, filed April 13, 1903, and issued August 2, 1904.

14. Hazel-Atlas, *A Book of Recipes*, 1924, 5. The company claimed use of the term E-Z Seal by 1904, and as early as 1896 (Lockhart et al., "Hazel-Atlas"; Toulouse, *Fruit Jars*). Hazel-Atlas production plants were

located in West Virginia, Pennsylvania, Alabama, Ohio, Indiana, Illinois, Michigan, Oklahoma, and California, and the company had sales offices in Chicago, Cleveland, Rochester, Philadelphia, New York City, Baltimore, and San Francisco (Weiskircher, "Hazel-Atlas").

15. Hazel-Atlas, *A Book of Recipes*, 1924, 14–25. A *Ball Blue Book* instruction manual produced in 1921 or 1922 also includes recipes for brains, head cheese, and cakes of sausage packed in their own pan grease (processed in a water bath for 1.5 hours), but doesn't compare this product to other strategies (Ball Brothers Glass Manufacturing Company, *The Ball Blue Book of Canning and Preserving Recipes*, edition M [Chicago: R. R. Donnelley and Sons, c1921–1922], 37. Folder 10, Box 1, Ball Corporation Collection 98.37, The Minnetrista Heritage Collection, Muncie, Indiana). By 1926, the N edition of Ball's cookbook included brains and "pork sausage" in its "special recipes" section—but has no recipe for head cheese and advocates processing pre-cooked sausage cakes, without the addition of lard, for 3.5 hours in a water bath, or 60 minutes at 15 pounds of pressure (Ball Brothers Company, *The Ball Blue Book of Canning and Preserving Recipes*, edition N [South Bend: L. P. Hardy Co., 1926], 19. Folder 10, Box 1, Ball Corporation Collection 98.37, The Minnetrista Heritage Collection, Muncie, Indiana).

16. "FAQs," *Photographic Reference Guide: Ball Fruit Jars*, www .fruitjar.org/ballweb/main.htm.

17. "Home," *The X-Files*, season 4, episode 2, 1996. Directed by Kim Manners, written by Glen Morgan and James Wong. The episode carried a viewer discretion warning.

18. Sigmund Freud, "The Uncanny," in *The Standard Edition of the Complete Psychological Works of Sigmund Freud*, ed. and trans. James Strachey, vol. 17 (London: Hogarth, 1953), 219–52; David B. Morris, "Gothic Sublimity," *New Literary History* 16, no. 2 (1985): 299–319; Brian McCuskey, "Not at Home: Servants, Scholars, and the Uncanny," *PMLA* 121, no. 2 (2006): 421–36.

19. Danille Elise Christensen, "Still Working: Performing Productivity through Gardening and Home Canning," in *The Expressive Lives of Elders*, ed. Jon Kay (Bloomington: Indiana University Press, 2018), 106–37.

20. Allen Batteau, *The Invention of Appalachia* (Tucson: University of Arizona Press, 1990); Emily M. Satterwhite, "The Politics of Hillbilly Horror," in *Navigating Souths: Transdisciplinary Explorations of a US Region*, ed. Michele Grigsby Coffey and Jodi Skipper (Athens: University of Georgia Press, 2017), 227–45; Nina Silber, "'What Does America Need So Much as Americans?': Race and Northern Reconciliation with Southern Appalachia, 1870–1900," in *Appalachians and Race: The*

Mountain South from Slavery to Segregation, ed. John Inscoe (Lexington: University Press of Kentucky, 2001), 245–58; Henry D. Shapiro, *Appalachia on Our Mind: The Southern Mountains and Mountaineers in the American Consciousness, 1870–1920* (Chapel Hill: University of North Carolina Press, 1978); Darlene Wilson, "The Felicitous Convergence of Mythmaking and Capital Accumulation: John Fox Jr. and the Formation of An(Other) Almost-White American Underclass," *Journal of Appalachian Studies* 1 (Fall 1995): 5–44, and "A Judicious Combination of Incident and Psychology: John Fox Jr. and the Southern Mountaineer Motif," in *Confronting Appalachian Stereotypes: Back Talk from an American Region*, ed. Dwight B. Billings, Gurney Norman, and Katherine Ledford (Lexington: University Press of Kentucky, 1999), 98–118.

21. Daniel Lindsey Thomas and Lucy Blayney Thomas, *Kentucky Superstitions* (Princeton, NJ: Princeton University Press, 1920), 5; McCuskey, "Not at Home," 424.

22. Ralph A. Pelton, "A Race of Rip Van Winkles Is Waking Up," *World Outlook* 5, no. 11 (1919): 20–32; "The Southern Highlanders Wake Up, but Still Make Corn 'Likker,'" *Literary Digest* 65, no. 1 (April 3, 1920): 56, 58.

23. Carrie Severt, interview by Geraldine Johnson, September 13, 1978, Blue Ridge Parkway Folklife Collection (AFC 1982/009), AFS 21,484 (BR8-GJ-R48), American Folklife Center, Library of Congress, Washington, D.C. Arlene Chaney, interview by Chelsea Bicknell, June 21, 2012, Folder 10, Box 1, Appalachian Foodways Oral History Collection (SAA 164), Berea College Special Collections & Archives, Berea, KY, 14–20. On enactments of humility and solidarity more generally, see Jane Greer, "Expanding Working-Class Rhetorical Traditions: The Moonlight Schools and Alternative Solidarities among Appalachian Women, 1911–1920," *College English* 77, no. 3 (2015): 216–35; Anita Puckett, *Seldom Ask, Never Tell: Labor and Discourse in Appalachia* (New York: Oxford University Press, 2000); Patricia Sawin, *Listening for a Life: A Dialogic Ethnography of Bessie Eldreth through Her Songs and Stories* (Logan: Utah State University Press, 2004).

24. Elizabeth Silverthorne, "Clover," *Legends and Lore of Texas Wildflowers* (College Station: Texas A&M University Press, 1996), 33–36; "Trifolium," *Native American Ethnobotany Database*, University of Michigan–Dearborn, 2017, http://naeb.brit.org/uses/search/?string=trifolium; Roy Vickery, "Clover (*Trifolium* spp.)," *Oxford Dictionary of Plant-Lore* (New York: Oxford University Press, 1997), 71–76; Thomas and Thomas, *Kentucky Superstitions*.

25. "Goldenrod School: Birthplace of 4-H" (trifold brochure), "A Tribute to Jessie Field Shambaugh" (magazine article, circa 1971), and corn sheller label, all at Goldenrod School and Nodaway Valley Historical Museum, Clarinda, Iowa; Tom Longden, "Jessie Field Shambaugh," DesMoinesRegister.Com, 2017, http://data.desmoinesregister.com/famous-iowans/jessie-field-shambaugh.

26. McKimmon, *When We're Green*, 44.

27. Weiskircher, "Hazel-Atlas"; "The Bottle Industry," 193.

28. Weiskircher, "Hazel-Atlas."

29. Wallace Stevens, "Anecdote of the Jar," in *The Collected Poems of Wallace Stevens* (New York: Alfred A. Knopf, 1990); "On 'Anecdote of the Jar,'" *Modern American Poetry*, http://www.english.illinois.edu/maps/poets/s_z/stevens/jar.htm; Kevin O'Donnell, "'Like Nothing Else in Tennessee': Wallace Stevens' 'Anecdote of the Jar,' Elizabethton, Tennessee, and the Industrial Logging of Appalachia," paper presented at the annual meeting of the Appalachian Studies Association (Huntington, WV, March 2014). Some have speculated that the poem refers to a fruit jar made by Dominion Glass, though this is unlikely given that Dominion was a Canadian firm and there were so many other locally produced fruit jars on the market in 1918.

30. Conn, *Beneficence*. At its height in 1951, Hazel-Atlas Glass Company employed five thousand and had thirteen factories across the country, with thirty-three glass tanks among them; in 1956, the company was purchased by Continental Can Company, and by 1964 most plants had been sold to Brockway Glass Company. In 1966, the Continental Can Company donated the main Hazel-Atlas building in Wheeling to West Liberty State College, and in 1972 it became the property of West Virginia Northern Community College. Employees attributed the decline and closure of the company to "managers who became complacent, took large profits in salaries, and failed to re-invest in research and development" (Lockhart et al., "Hazel-Atlas"; Weiskircher, "Hazel-Atlas"; Joan Weiskircher, "Hazel Atlas Glass History," *West Virginia Northern Community College*, 2016, http://www.wvncc.edu/alumni/hazel-atlas-glass-history/105).

31. Bill Lockhart, Beau Schriever, Carol Serr, and Bill Lindsey, "Federal Glass Co.," in *Encyclopedia of Manufacturer's Marks on Glass Containers*, comp. and ed. Bottle Research Group, vol. F–G, July 8, 2015, Society for Historical Archaeology, Historic Glass Bottle Identification & Information Website, https://sha.org/bottle/pdffiles/FederalGlass.pdf.

Chapter 12

Cornbread and *Fabada:* Savoring a West Virginia Story

Suronda Gonzalez

MY MOTHER, Sandra (Coffman) Gonzalez, is the youngest of nine children born and raised on a sprawling 188-acre farm in Braxton County, West Virginia. Her family history, which traces its roots back to the American Revolution, is the typical narrative of white, Anglo-Saxon, Protestant rural farmers in the state. She and her siblings were born in clusters of three—first girls, then boys, then girls again. Farming was their life, and their daily survival depended on the gifts born from the land. In addition to the many animals they relied on for eggs, milk, meat, and labor, they planted a broad assortment of crops. From the ridge and the holler, they gathered luscious fruits from the apple, peach, and pear orchards. Despite moving from the farm more than fifty years ago, the seasons are still deeply ingrained in my mother's memory. Several years ago, when editing a document organized by berry seasons, I called her to help me correlate the fruit harvests to specific months so I could reconstruct a reliable timeline. As I expected, she rattled them off by heart and questioned why I didn't inherently know this myself.

What I hadn't realized at the time was just how dependent her family was on the land and its bounty. As a young girl, my mother and her siblings, along with my grandparents and extended family, worked long hours. Hoeing one row of corn took an entire morning. Upon completing one row, they found shade in the expansive field and enjoyed a biscuit lunch. After a brief rest, they continued their work and often did not return home for supper until after dark. The harvest season was no less labor intensive and required a coordinated response to preserve, through canning and drying, everything they produced. It was their insurance against hunger knocking at their door during the winter.

The cellar was a showcase for the family's hard work. My mother can recall with a sense of satisfaction the delectable array of colors lining the walls: stone jars with pickled corn, pickled beans, and pickled cucumbers; glass jars with strawberry, raspberry, blackberry, and gooseberry jams; and larger vessels filled with green beans, tomatoes, and corn; as well as the potato bins that included her favorite sweet potatoes and the strings of drying apples that would be used for holiday pies. Eating at a restaurant was so unusual that my mother remembers how her sister-in-law, then working as a waitress in nearby Summersville, treated her to a piece of graham cracker pie when the family stopped in while on an errand in town.

Like many in rural West Virginia, the family eked out a living by working above and below the earth. While her mother and siblings ran the farm, her father sometimes logged but also ventured underground to mine. This work, already taxing, was especially difficult since he had several disabilities. His mother had accidentally dropped him in the fireplace as an infant. The burns left him badly scarred, blind in one eye, and with debilitating emotional effects from the head injury. As the strain of making ends meet mounted, it took a toll on his already compromised health. My grandmother discovered that although my grandfather would head off to work every morning with the lunch she had lovingly packed, sometimes he never made it to work. Instead, he would walk a mile or so to a large field where he would sit under a tree all morning, eat his lunch in the afternoon, and then return home. When I find myself romanticizing about an idyllic farming existence, I remember how it broke him and the ways its demands stole opportunities from his children and grandchildren.

While my mother grew up in the region's open spaces, my father, Ronald Gonzalez, an only child, grew up in the shadow of the zinc factory in the Harrison County town of Spelter, West Virginia. The turn-of-the-twentieth-century immigrant narrative with new arrivals entering through Ellis Island, though not generally associated with Appalachia, belongs to his side of my family. In the early 1900s, low fuel prices in the state spurred industrial growth and a demand for laborers. Italian immigrants arrived to work in the coal mines, while Spaniards in north-central West Virginia worked almost exclusively in metallurgy. In fact, industrialists planning to establish zinc works in the state went directly to the mineral-rich province of Asturias in northern Spain to recruit laborers from the booming industry there.

My paternal grandfather came from Asturias to the United States as a toddler in 1914. At around age sixteen, he began working in the factory alongside his father and their Spanish immigrant neighbors. Many of the families knew each other since they had lived and worked together in their hometowns before emigrating. Güela's (my paternal grandmother's) father had also been lured from Asturias by recruiters promising good-paying jobs and an escape from mandatory military service. At one point, there were about 1,500 Spanish families living in Harrison County, enough to have a Vice Consulate in the county seat.

Adding the forty-six years my father worked in the factory to those worked by his father and grandfathers, the men in my direct family line put in more than two hundred cumulative years in the zinc industry in West Virginia alone. Others with Asturian roots in the United States share a similar history. I quickly found that by connecting regions of the United States that smelted zinc (Cherryvale, Kansas; Donora, Pennsylvania; Canton, Ohio; Fairmont City, Missouri) or by following EPA Superfund sites, I could also find Spaniards from Asturias. While knowledge of the "zinc belt" has faded into the past, those who lived and worked in Spelter knew it well. It connected them to family and friends. Some had traveled to other zinc belt locales before ending up in West Virginia, while others traveled back and forth between sites to keep steady work. My father left the Spelter factory when it closed in 2001 and although the site has been razed, it still looms large—through my father's serious health issues, the lingering environmental concerns in our community, and the ways zinc smelting connects descendants across the country.

In the Spelter of my father's youth, daily life revolved around two sounds—the factory whistle and the school bell. Far removed from the rural experience of my mother's family, Güela once told me how my father, as a youngster visiting a farm for the first time, refused a glass of fresh milk with the indignant response, "We don't drink milk from cows. We drink milk from the store." While brothers and fathers went off to the factory or the mines, Spanish women and their Italian women neighbors tended to the endless duties of housekeeping and child rearing. They earned extra money by taking in boarders as well as doing cleaning and laundry for the bosses' families. Industrial life, while different from farming and mining, was also dirty, debilitating, and draining.

As Catholics and as immigrants, my Spanish family experienced the jeers and intimidation tactics of their white, native-born neighbors. My paternal grandfather, Güelo, recalled a day in the early 1920s when he came upon a burning cross at the border of another Asturian enclave in Annmore, West Virginia. He had intended to walk to a nearby fair, but to his surprise Ku Klux Klan members in full regalia patrolled the border and chased him back to "his side of town." As a youngster, I heard Güela's shock and fear at discovering a KKK pillow among the others on a neighbor's sofa and how my family had even witnessed a cross burning in Spelter.

When my parents began dating in the early 1960s, the deep-seated racial and ethnic tensions were still very visible. So-called sundown towns in West Virginia were effective in marking white-only spaces. My father vividly recalls that while on his way to visit my mother's parents for the first time, he passed a sign warning blacks, in explicitly racist language, to get out of town before dark. He understood that the message was meant for him too.

As poor white families living and working in Spelter benefited from linguistic and race privilege, some chose to intimidate and jeer at their immigrant neighbors. Perhaps as a means of survival, rebellion, simple ignorance, or some combination of all three, Spaniards and Italians in the area developed their own racial and class prejudices. They insultingly labeled their white, Anglo neighbors "snuffies." *Merriam-Webster* notes that the term refers to someone who is snobby.[1] To descendants of immigrant families in north-central West Virginia, however, it means the exact opposite.

The term is most likely rooted in the characters of the *Snuffy Smith* comic strips of the 1930s. Cartoonist Billy DeBeck's image of the Smith family represents well-known stereotypes of "hillbillies": uneducated, racist, lazy, poor, in overalls and shoeless.[2] Men in the strip are fond of hunting, fishing, and tipping a jug of shine made from their still on the hill, while the women spend their days gossiping, raising the young'uns and trying to tame the menfolk. Rather than rejecting the portrayal as an ugly stereotype put upon their native-born neighbors, much like they themselves had been wrongly labeled and marginalized, immigrants in the community embraced the term. In reinforcing community divisions, they, like their white, working-class neighbors, diminished their effectiveness in confronting the structural forces responsible for keeping workers separated and wages low.

Many of the Asturians' complaints about their poor white neighbors revolved around food. They would describe, with much disgust, how they had witnessed someone put catsup on *chorizo*—a great sin. Or, like the image made famous during Eleanor Roosevelt's visit to West Virginia, their neighbors would eat cornflakes for dinner. In addition to their offensive food habits, poor working Appalachians were also portrayed as having no "gracia," or what my immigrant family considered "grace" and "hospitality." For my Asturian family, food was part of hosting, celebration, and ritual. It was an integral part of community and culture. For the native-born Anglo side of my family, food represented a necessary fuel for a hard day's work. It conjured the physical world associated with hunger, farming, and the kitchen.

The stark contrast in my family's racial, religious, and ethnic identities, like the differences between their rural and industrial upbringings, was bridged only by the commonality of poverty. Longtime Appalachians and Spanish immigrants alike relied on locally grown foodstuffs to supplement their meager wages. Like my native-born grandparents, my Spanish grandparents gardened. It was part of their daily routine in Spelter, just as it had been in the Old World. They planted leafy greens. Key among these was kale, an essential ingredient for the delicious soups, especially *fabada* (bean soup) that contained bits of *chorizo* (Spanish pork sausage flavored with paprika) and a touch of *morcilla* (sausage made with pork fat, pork blood, and onions) for special flavor. When a cousin visited from Spain in the 1970s, a rare and special occasion, she traveled the many miles and through airport customs with a basket of locally grown dried beans and *jamón* (cured ham). While one could make do with local varieties in West Virginia, the familiar texture and specific flavors from Asturias were unparalleled. While we can't travel through airports with jamón any longer, beans and saffron are still frequently requested as souvenirs to bring back home after trips to Asturias from the United States.

In addition to bringing familiar foods to the table, gardening brought a sense of pride that sometimes turned into friendly competition among immigrant neighbors. To get anything to grow in nutrient-poor soil contaminated by elements from factory smoke took a great deal of care and attention. (In 2011, as a result of a class-action lawsuit, the town and surrounding areas of Spelter were awarded $34 million to clean up the heavy metal contamination.) Long after the company had sold houses to individuals, and long after the first generation of workers had retired, my great-uncle bragged to his Spanish buddies about the richness of the garden at his new home a few miles away. He crowed that he had juicy red tomatoes as early as June. Not one to admit defeat, even in the face of such a bold lie, he spent hours in the afternoon sun sewing store-bought tomatoes onto the vines when his friends had demanded to see the evidence. He volunteered to drive them himself and quieted their disbelief with a brief gander from the car window in a very quick drive-by.

The relationship between my paternal grandmother and my mother represents the common threads of what I long understood as two distinct and disconnected stories. My mother was an outsider and suspect on several levels. Her deep knowledge of gardening and her real interest in cooking, coupled with her love for Güela's only child, gave her a unique entrée into her mother-in-law's kitchen—and eventually her heart. Güela knew that my mother was the closest thing she would have to a daughter. And when my mother showed an interest in the special dishes she prepared, Güela put her to work. In my mother's mind, tortilla Española (a traditional and simple omelet of potatoes, eggs, and onions) must have been reminiscent of the home fried potatoes she had grown up with on the farm, and fabada was simply a spicier version of navy beans and ham so familiar to her. Both foods were readily available, cheap, and kept the belly full. As my mother and Güela worked together in the kitchen they uncovered common connections that resulted in a lasting, true affection.

As a young child, even I was given an important role in helping with the customary midday Sunday meal at Güela and Güelo's house. The routine began in the early morning, and I remember waking up to the wonderful smells emanating from the kitchen. Dinner was served at two o'clock and the family's morning

schedules revolved around that event. Güelo and I were charged
with heading off to Marty Defazio's bakery on Route 19 to fetch a
loaf of his renowned hard-crusted Italian bread. A trip that could
have taken at most fifteen minutes usually took more than an hour.
The slippery feel of flour dusting the floor of the bakery was a de-
light, and the workers would put on a show as they made my special
loaf, moving dough from tub, to table, to oven and finally to a rack to
cool before it was placed in the white bag for the short trip home.

By the time we returned home, my grandmother and mother
would be putting the final touches on the Sunday meal, which
usually included *arroz con pollo* (chicken and rice) or *cocico* (stew).
I remember my grandparents observing the Catholic tradition
of meatless Fridays and other Holy Days, with tuna empanadas
(meat pies) or fish that my Güelo had caught. Christmas Eve and
Christmas Day dinners were the most special meals of the year.
Over the years, my mother watched and learned, being sure to
carefully note which pots and pans were reserved for which
dishes. Beyond the main courses, my mother took in the secrets
of making sweets including *bollinas* (fried dough with nuts, sugar,
and sometimes custard) as well as *brazo Gitano* (literally "gypsy
arm," a delicate sponge cake lathered with egg custard and toasted
almonds). By her early twenties, my mother knew how to prepare
the customary dishes of her family and those of her immigrant
in-laws and extended family as well. Many have testified to the
fact that her empanada is as good as their grandmother's, and to
the chagrin of many daughters of those original Spanish immigrants, it is admittedly better than theirs.

Today, Güela's special pots and pans reside in my mother's
kitchen. They were key to continuing our Spanish traditions and
no one was willing to take the risk of trying another newer pan,
for fear that the recipe would turn out differently. In addition to
being the keeper of Spanish food traditions, my mother is also the
guardian of all the farming and canning skills, as well as of the
"country" recipes from her family. I can correlate a particular pan
to its dish but can go no further. Yet, the family recipes, even if

they were written down, cannot be replicated without the knowing hand and eye that my mother gleaned from watching my grand-mothers. Through her hands, the wisdom of my grandparents and the generations before them, native-born and immigrant alike, has been passed down. It is part of a common Appalachian legacy of resourcefulness, love of family, and a celebration of persistence.

NOTES

1. *Merriam-Webster*, s.v. "snuffy (*adj.*)," accessed September 2, 2018, https://www.merriam-webster.com/dictionary/snuffy.

2. See Anthony Harkins, *Hillbilly: A Cultural History of an American Icon* (New York: Oxford University Press, 2004), 103–40.

Chapter 13

Haute Appalachia: Wine and Wine Tourism

Jessie Blackburn and William Schumann

DRIVE DOWN the spine of today's Central Appalachia and take
a head count of the number of interstate exits demarcated with a
cluster of grapes. Spot the signs with arrows pointing drivers north,
south, east, and west toward wineries and vineyards. Follow these
signs and head deep into Appalachia's wine country: terroir dotted
with converted barns, farmhouses, and manors turned into tasting
rooms surrounded by combinations of steep and gentle mountainside vineyards. What fascinates us about these old mountains
and wide valleys that open up into hundreds of acres under vine
and the tasting rooms is the bravery that it takes to be a vintner
right now, right here. In addition to oenological and viticultural
expertise, it takes bravery to decide to plant a grapevine in these

mountains, wait up to five years to find out if it took, ferment and bottle the juice, and hope that true wine critics (and the average wine tourist) will find you and your wine and know good wine when they taste it—despite the relative newness of Appalachia as a credible contender in the modern world of wine. We saw this bravery in a young farmer-turned-vintner who hopes wine will be the thing that allows him to hang onto his great-grandfather's farm. We saw it in the retired scientist who returned home to turn her family's land into a vineyard in order to apply her science background to grape cultivation and fermentation. We saw it in the Italian winemaker who left Italy to gamble on Appalachian terroir as the "new frontier" for winemaking instead of relocating to the tried-and-true and glutted regions of Napa or Sonoma. We saw it in the winemaker who turned an old cabin into a tasting room and planted acres of Petit Manseng, Cabernet Sauvignon, and American Norton to satisfy the tastes of sweet and dry wine drinkers alike. Indeed, from southwestern New York State to northeastern Alabama, Appalachian wine country is filled with as much risk as expertise as vintners increasingly invest in the region's physical and cultural terroir.

Appalachian winemakers have to contend with more than the varying soil, climate, and elevation (all of which make up the physical terroir of place). As much as wine depends on its natural environment and material terroir, wine drinkers depend on their presumptions about the wine region attached to that terroir. This means that as Appalachian winemakers harness their bravery to plant their first grapevines, they must also prepare to navigate wine drinkers' tastes in wine as well as their cultural presumptions about Appalachia. So how exactly has today's burgeoning Appalachian wine region come to see itself and be seen by its wine lovers? As an anthropologist and a cultural rhetorician in the field of Appalachian studies and as avid wine drinkers, we are drawn to figure this out. As such, we took a few years to make our way up and down the region's wine trails (spanning over one thousand miles)—tasting and interviewing as we visited over seventy Appalachian wineries.

Haute Appalachia: Wine and Wine Tourism

Beyond the quality of the wine, which is increasingly recognized in national and international wine competitions, we
looked at visual, textual, and spatial rhetorics of Appalachian
wine tourism to examine how Appalachian vintners connect
to—and ultimately market—their local and regional ideas of
place. We entered into this work seeing the Appalachian winery
much in the same way that cultural rhetoricians see spaces as
"an important node in a series of difficulties and possibilities that
characterize the contemporary moment, in particular the difficult
contradictions between global and local, spectacle and authenticity, consumer culture and individual identities."[1] We considered
how wines are named, labels are designed, tasting sheets are
written, landscapes and architectures are situated, tasting rooms
are laid out and decorated, and wine tastings are performed as
"Appalachian." Through it all, we found that while not all wineries
in Appalachia rhetorically position themselves as Appalachian,
those that do must balance global narratives of wine-as-refinement
with regional narratives of mountain rusticity and the rural idyll.
Appalachian food and drink and wines "can be used to create a
connection, to create a sense of identity and identification, and
to perform culture," as southern foodways scholars Ashli Quesinberry Stokes and Wendy Atkins-Sayre put it. Often in Appalachian wine country, aesthetics of rusticity are performed in ways
that enable the region's vintners to reach wine tourists through rhetorical moves that tap into—indeed, market—vineyard experiences
that embody and then invert popular notions of Appalachian
qualities: agrarian, bucolic, relaxed, down-home, invitational,
slow-paced, and nostalgic. Through rusticity, many vineyards
create a class-based counternarrative that taps into a commodified
performativity of the gentleman farmer and relies on the leisure
class's popular (if not long-standing) conspicuous consumption of
the rural.[2]

The Appalachian wine industry is growing at an exponential
rate. Some point to this as a long-overdue rebound, as Virginia
and North Carolina led Appalachia in the number of established

wineries throughout the region until Prohibition in the 1920s, which brought the region's winemaking to a standstill and shut down production nationwide. Estimates of the number of wineries in today's Appalachia vary, but we counted over four hundred during more than thirty months of our fieldwork, which began in 2015 and remains ongoing. Our count includes a few winery areas located just outside the Appalachian Regional Commission's (ARC) geographic designation of the region but well within the geological footprint of the Appalachians. We conducted seventy-five site visits and over fifty interviews and reviewed over 250 Appalachian winery websites. Given the growth of the industry, we kept asking the question: What makes a winery "Appalachian"? What we found is that regional wineries that connect themselves to Appalachian identities do so through the use of textual, visual, material, and cultural rhetorics. Specifically, we use *cultural rhetorics* to mean "understanding a specific culture's systems, beliefs, relationships to the past, practices of meaning-making, and practices of carrying culture forward to future generations."[3] Appalachian wineries don't have to look far to find the region's relationship to past practices and customs associated with winemaking.

Though there are few examples of native viticulture today (Appalachian North Carolina's Native Vines is one example), Appalachian grape cultivation began before European colonization. And coastal North Carolina is home to America's oldest cultivated grapevine, the Mothervine, which is a muscadine vine discovered in 1584. The region's wine industry also has deep roots, with Virginia's wine history tracing back to Thomas Jefferson and his experiments with *vitis vinifera* (European grapes) and native grapes in his Monticello vineyards of Appalachia's Shenandoah Valley. Nineteenth-century industrialization and migration introduced more European peoples and viticultural traditions to Appalachia, including Italian and German knowledge of wine and grapes. Before Prohibition, commercial wineries operated in several Appalachian states, and southwestern New York was an early hotbed of production by the mid-1800s.[4]

Prohibition ended all that; however, folks continued making homemade Appalachian fruit wines—using everything from wild grapes to pawpaws—for generations. After the repeal of Prohibition, commercial production did not return to northern Appalachia until the 1950s and '60s and to Appalachian Virginia and North Carolina until the late 1970s and '80s. Yet some Appalachian wineries, such as the Dr. Konstantin Frank Winery in Hammondsport, New York; Wills Creek Vineyards in Attalla, Alabama; and Barboursville Vineyards in Barboursville, Virginia, draw directly from European winemaking experience today. Perhaps just as important as a particular winemaking background, commercial wine production since Prohibition has been shaped by state-level policies and local cultural politics about wine. Not surprisingly, we learned that each Appalachian state has a different policy approach to supporting that state's wine industry. For instance, the growth of Virginia wineries can be traced to high-level cooperation and strategic planning over time among wineries and wine associations, state tourism authorities, agricultural and extension agencies, and supportive legislators; in contrast, Alabama's wineries have largely operated according to restrictive policies put in place at the end of Prohibition, such as multiple levels of taxation and distribution regulations that curtail growth.[5]

Basic issues like determining whether wine should be supported under a state's agricultural or tourism bureaucracy have wide-ranging impacts on the production, distribution, marketing, and promotion of regional wine. Local cultural politics influence some of these decisions, too. For example, we visited a rural Tennessee vintner who had to overcome local government efforts to effectively outlaw his winery by rewriting zoning laws. We saw biblical quotations about wine displayed in a West Virginia winery to preempt public inquiries about the morality of drinking wine. In short, successful wine tourism involves more than just viticulture, and this complexity is what drives our research.

What grabs our attention in Appalachian wine and wine tourism's cultural rhetorics is how wineries navigate the

expectations of global wine communities and simultaneously in-
corporate locality, or place, into these narratives. Wine and wine
tourism specifically are global phenomena, which means that any
single winery visit anticipates broader expectations about quality,
taste, and experience. More often than not, these expectations
reference "Old World" and "New World" wines, which indicate
both geographic spaces for and ideas about experiencing "authentic" wine. Appalachian rhetorics of place sometimes overlap with
ideas of the Old World, particularly notions of a romanticized
rusticity: both, in effect, are timeless and authentic in compari-
son to mainstream American culture. Just as often, however,
Appalachia can conjure negative stereotypes of the chronically
backwoods and unrefined, which—when considered in terms of
wine rhetorics—often translate into public perceptions about wine
quality. In terms of wine tourism, this narrative framing anticipates public expectations of the Appalachian vineyard experience.
Not all wineries in Appalachia position themselves as Appalachian: some are über-modern and intentionally evacuated of any
regional reference points; others mimic older European architecture and cultural rhetorics. However, of the wineries that *do* claim
Appalachia, each must decide how to balance narratives of refine-
ment with rusticity (i.e., the "posh rural") to create a wine-tasting
and vineyard/winery *experience* that resonates with broader wine
tourism expectations and, most obviously, encourages wine sales.
So, how does one combine haute couture and down-home aesthetics to sell wine?

Our travels have shown that there are a wide variety of
responses to this question. As much as it is about material terroir
and successful farming, winemaking in Appalachia relies on selling
place as an immediately local experience. As one Yadkin Valley,
North Carolina, vintner shared with us, one must create heritage
as "something that comes from the soil to the table." Cultivating
that regional connection is done in a variety of ways. Collectively,
these elements of the "wine experience" shape the aesthetics of
selling wine as an Appalachian phenomenon.

MAKING WINE "APPALACHIAN"

One of the obvious ways to announce a winery's commitment to Appalachian locality is through the design of the building and tasting room. We visited renovated mills, an old jail, log-cabin homesteads, repurposed barns, replica Italian chalets and French chateaus, converted farmhouses, mobile homes, cinder-block buildings, redeveloped storefronts, and corrugated metal box structures. These facilities were variously surrounded by rolling vineyards; mountain views; streams; rivers; ponds; forests; flowering fields; the Blue Ridge Parkway; the Appalachian Trail and other trailways, highways and interstates; middle-class subdivisions; downtown districts; and Christmas tree farms. In all cases, though, space is used as a way to indicate *place* in response to the understanding that tourists are searching for what rhetoric scholar Greg Dickinson calls "spaces that seem authentic or real. These spaces provide the visual and the material resources with which individuals can attempt to negotiate the fragmentation and destabilization that characterize their cultural context."[6] While some of the region's wineries ignore or counter the plebeian stereotypes that prescribe cultural narratives about Appalachian place, we also see many wineries that acknowledge the storied past by invoking and sometimes re-inscribing variations of a mountain narrative.

Perhaps the most iconic combination of Appalachia's buildings and settings is the farmhouse and farm, which actually vary in style and purpose from one end of the region to the other. In fact, it's quite common for regional wineries and vineyards to label themselves a "farm and vineyard." What is interesting about the farmhouses we visited is that while some were homesteads original to the farm-turned-vineyard, others were neither original nor pretending to be. We identified three primary types of farmhouse wineries: (1) those that build traditional farmhouses but for the sole purpose of the winery; (2) those that reference the farmhouse design and feel but favor other building materials (e.g., corrugated metal); and (3) those that restore or repurpose authentic farmhouses or other bona fide period buildings into tasting rooms and event facilities.

For example, Cavender Creek Vineyards and Winery, located along the Dahlonega Wine Trail in the north Georgia mountains, features a hand-hewn log cabin dating back to the 1820s. This cabin served as the original tasting room for the winery, but it now sits as the "cabin among the vines" and serves as a bed-and-breakfast in the middle of the vineyard along with free-ranging chickens, farm dogs, and donkeys. Though the owner built a new tasting room, it is constructed to emulate a cabin—replete with the wide front porch, reclaimed siding, traditional metal roof, and hardwood floors throughout.

In the mountains of Nebo, North Carolina, sits South Creek Vineyards and Winery, with its vineyard surrounding a hundred-year-old farmhouse. With a portion of the first floor sectioned off to serve as the tasting room, the vintners live in the substantial farmhouse appointed with yellow clapboard siding, traditional farmhouse shutters, numerous chimneys, and an iconic wrap-around porch. Situated alongside this farmhouse is a traditional red barn, but what makes this barn especially interesting is the oversized barn quilt of a grape cluster mounted near the pitch of the barn's roof. This image, along with the vines and the farmhouse in the distance, creates a visual narrative framed in sentimental rhetorics of rusticity, tradition, heritage, and culture. However, with the inclusion of an iconic barn quilt of grape clusters, we see a new element injected into that narrative through a remixing of traditional folk art.

In contrast, Pippin Hill Farm and Vineyards, a newly constructed farmhouse and adjacent 3,600-square-foot granary, sits in the middle of a rolling mountainside vineyard on the Monticello Wine Trail near Charlottesville, Virginia. Brand new, yet built to look old and restored, this vineyard aims for posh rusticity on a grand scale—turning iconic symbols of agricultural labor into signifiers of the leisure class, the rural idyll, and conspicuous consumption. Pippin Hill's virtual photo gallery features images invoking croquet, garden strolls, fox hunting, and equestrian sports. A farmhouse aesthetic is created for weddings, events, and large tasting groups through the use of clapboard siding; traditional, narrow, double-hung windows; reclaimed hardwood and stone floors; oversized farm-harvest tables; small accent windows in the gables; and oversized doorways that lead from the tasting room onto the stone veranda, into the granary, and out into the potager garden. This winery gives an impression of a stunningly well maintained structure that has been passed down from heir to heir. Indeed, it is a total luxury build that turns symbols of agriculture and the laboring class into signifiers of the gentleman farmer. These structures have never functioned as anything other than a setting for a tasting room and wedding events, yet the visual rhetoric invokes a sense of *restored* place and history through its structural nostalgia, its bucolic grandeur, and its spirit of opulence. While the other examples of farmhouse rhetorics invoke the roots of a farming tradition or laboring-class background, this winery and others similar to it, such as Early Mountain Vineyards in Madison, Virginia, illustrate an alternative rhetoric: these forms of nostalgic pastoralism suggest a history of farm *manors* more than of farm *houses*.

Appalachian winery decor also varies, but wood and metal motifs abound across winery architectures and styles. "Shabby chic" exposed wood is particularly common, ranging from rustic and reclaimed floors to tree trunk supports to finished beams and detailed woodwork. In one instance, Whitebarrel Winery outside Blacksburg, Virginia, uses reclaimed wooden shipping pallets as wall art. In other examples, we find old farm implements, cooking utensils, and industrial lighting adding rusticity to walls and corners. At vineyards such as Homeplace Vineyard in Chatham, Virginia; Elkin Creek Vineyard in Elkin, North Carolina; or Heston Farm Vineyards in Fairmont, West Virginia, we find antique furniture on display—both well-preserved and rough and worn. Some of these features are in former farmhouses, but others are found inside metal and block buildings, including a few with indoor wood structures with sheet metal roofs (i.e., interior barns). Metal is a common complement to wood: wrought iron, copper, and tin chandeliers, door handles, and wall art (e.g., rusty signs) add to the rural rhetorics on display. Tasting rooms often combine these elements with striking success in creating rough, glossy, polished, or natural wood tasting bars.

We met winemakers who fashion this aesthetic from their own farming heritage, and we met others who paid international consultants to help them achieve an Appalachian aesthetic based on visual symbols that simulate just enough rusticity (a near fetishization of the gentleman farmer) to invoke bucolic nostalgia but not so much as to signify a "working-class awareness of wine" (as one winemaker described this tenuous balance). This working-class awareness of wine is complicated, but for many winemakers, it means avoiding the wines of the "unsophisticated" palate. Obviously a loaded, class-based claim of aesthetics, the "unsophisticated palate," we came to understand, references wine drinkers who enjoy sweet wines and fruit wines, which some interviewees also described as "porch" wines, "bootlegger" wines, "grandma's" wine, or "kitchen" wines. Though the description of unsophisticated wines differed, anecdotally, the definition always involved references to the novice wines found throughout historic and/or current-day Appalachia.

One particularly winsome element many of the wineries share is an Appalachian farm winery dog as mascot. Some wineries even welcome well-behaved dogs as visitors to the grounds, which is unthinkable in many wine regions outside Appalachia. We've lost count of the number of satisfied vineyard dogs we encountered along the Appalachian wine trail. At the Carolina Heritage Vineyard and Winery in Elkin, North Carolina, we toured the vineyard in the farm truck with a dog riding shotgun in one of our laps while the other one of us rode in the bed of the truck beside a faithful mutt. Chloe, the iconic golden retriever, greeted us at the door of Jones von Drehle Vineyards and Winery in Thurmond, North Carolina. In Smithburg, Maryland, the hounds bayed in the background and ran the vines at Red Heifer Winery. Chateau Morrisette in Floyd, Virginia, hosts dog adoption days; dog profiles appear on their wine labels, with many of the wines named after favorite dogs; and the winery's dog policy invites well-behaved dogs on a leash to the winery courtyard, tasting patio, gazebos, Sunday Sounds on the Courtyard, and their Black Dog Music Festivals. In fact, throughout the region, it's worth watching your step to avoid tripping over the water bowls strewn across many winery porches. These vineyard dogs are found in off-the-beaten-path wineries; urban tasting rooms; understated wineries; sprawling vineyard estates; and established wine areas. We find images of the vineyard dogs on wine labels, with some wineries naming the vintner's choice after an especially beloved vineyard hound. We find wineries with websites featuring images of bird dogs and emulations of fox hunting on the vineyard grounds—simultaneously referencing class as well as a sentimentalism for rural retreats. These lovable totems invoke Appalachia's agricultural history as well as a truth that, despite wine's class-based mythos, winemaking starts with farming. Rhetorically, these moves enable Appalachian wineries to promote a no-fuss approach to wine tasting as an adjunct of accessing quality wine within pastoral, rustic mountain settings.

Place and wine are further intertwined through labeling, which is both a commercial art form and a means of preserving local memories and meanings. Several vintners use their wine labels to capitalize on their own agricultural heritage, and still more invoke Appalachia's farming traditions, including white and red blends labeled with images of tractors, cows, and barns. Even more prevalent are labels named after natural features and places, such as local waterways and mountains. Wineries claim attachments to material and cultural terroir vis-à-vis community histories and local knowledge. Label art supports these rhetorical strategies with stylized hills, rivers, flora, fauna, and (in one case) topographic maps. In these and other instances, we see label art serving as reference points to place in order to geographically anchor the winery as well as signify the wine tourist's vineyard experience. Labels serve as rhetorical framing for and aesthetic extensions of the winery's rusticity.

Beyond natural and local motifs, some wineries choose to appeal to cultural stereotypes through their labels or recycle one of rural Appalachia's most-stereotyped traditions: moonshining. Some of these wineries make distilled spirits, while others merely reference the history of illicit alcohol, occasionally naming wines after specific moonshine runs or local figures of the bootlegging past; a few even feature label art with visual references to the caricatured 'XXX Moonshine' or old-style liquor labels. We found that this strategy sometimes works well for the ethos of the winery, such as Calaboose Cellars in Andrews, North Carolina, selling "Revinoor's Red" and other wines out of a restored one-room, historic jailhouse.

Other wineries that invoke Appalachian rhetorics move in the opposite direction by presenting their wine and wine-tasting experience as highly refined and distinct from a low-folk Appalachian moonshining past, even going so far as to avoid vineyard events featuring local foods, art, and music so as to deter "those kinds of sweet wine drinkers," as one western Maryland winemaker explained when asked if he features traditional Appalachian music in weekly music events at the vineyard. This winemaker was careful to distinguish his wines and his winery from other nearby wineries that appeal to "that crowd" of unsophisticated drinkers looking more for a party wine than a fine bottle to take home and enjoy with a meal. He was careful to explain that live music in his vineyard is a trio of classical or jazz musicians—never bluegrass. When he pairs his wines with local farm goods, it is artisanal cheese and charcuterie— never barbecue or burgers. This winemaker chooses to attach his wines to Maryland's material terroir but not its cultural terroir, and this move is intentional in an attempt to distinguish his wines from other wines and wineries of the region that might not survive the test of time, cultural stigmas, or the discriminating wine critic.

Many wineries begin to make these distinctions not through labeling but in a commitment to making dry wine, sweet wine, or a mix of both. At stake is a consuming audience, and there are clear, if indirect, associations between class and the sweetness of wine. Predominantly dry wine–making wineries very often reference this audience as "educated wine drinkers" with a "sophisticated" palate, who make up vital customer bases (i.e., wine "weekenders") from cities such as Atlanta or Washington, D.C. Geared toward this target audience are the artisan events and food-and-wine tastings that many of the wineries hold—featuring local musicians, potters, and other artisans, while pairing wines with local artisanal cheeses, chocolates, and charcuterie as well as bringing in local food trucks serving regional and international cuisine. This nod to the eat-and-drink-local movement illustrates the region's ability to attach its agriculture and viticulture to its cuisine and culture in progressive-traditional ways that resonate with wine tourists seeking an experience of place when visiting wine country. Wineries also draw everyone from dedicated wine enthusiasts to wedding parties to local communities, so it is common to find at least some variety of style on many tasting room menus. Incidentally, some of the best makers of "educated wine" we met offered the unsolicited opinion that the sweetness of wine has little bearing on its quality, yet winemakers invariably acknowledged that many wine tourists buy bottles to take back home and share based on the notion that sharing wine with others can "serve as a symbol of the identity of the host, emphasizing his or her likes and dislikes, regional affiliation, class, gender, and so forth."[7] For many, dry is still considered refined, while sweet is considered to be for less-educated and, presumably, poorer and even more "local" consumers. We see wineries throughout the region making this taste distinction, with many wineries admitting that they have to keep something sweet in their portfolio to satisfy many of their local guests.

Even more fascinating is the number of times vintners shared with us that their dry wines are priced higher than their sweet wines, thereby fulfilling the popular notion that price indicates quality *especially* in moments of conspicuous consumption. The price point of dry versus sweet wine also illuminates the highbrow/lowbrow tensions associated with Appalachia's burgeoning wine industry. The same sentiment is found in the "argument that the vast majority of local food initiatives appeal only to those with the financial means to participate. As a result, these initiatives have been labeled as elitist, exclusive, and inequitable."[8] It comes as little surprise, then, that the region's wineries would be preoccupied with satisfying the wine *drinker* looking for a ten-dollar bottle of wine as well as the wine *critic* looking for a bottle with an elite price tag. What is fascinating, though, is how the price of a bottle signifies quality when, after all, wine is a matter of subjective taste.

At the core of Appalachia's best wineries is the truly essential element of success: good agricultural practices. And people are taking notice. In 2017, *The Daily Meal* rated the Shenandoah Valley's Barboursville Winery as the eighth-best winery in America.[9] Similar in terroir to Old World wine regions like Italy and France, Appalachia's altitudes, first and last frost dates, precipitation, humidity, downdraft and winds, and minerality enable the growth of *vitis vinifera* and American hybrid grapes. Appalachia's wine regions are quickly becoming known for high-quality and award-winning Viognier, Chardonnay, Pinot Grigio, sauvignon blanc, Vermentino, Petit Verdot, Petit Manseng, Chambourcin (a personal favorite of ours), Cabernet Franc, Seyval blanc, vidal blanc, Traminette, Chardonel, and others. More closely associated to Appalachia, if less respected in the popular culture of wine, are native varieties like Scuppernong and Muscadine, many of which defy popular expectations of good wine. The endless variations of climate, soil, and topography that define the region's possibilities of winemaking are increasingly formalized in an Appalachian network of American Viticultural Areas (AVAs) and an ever-growing number of wine trails. As a result, we are seeing a rise in demand for regionally grown grapes, and we are seeing a slow and steady growth of grapevines where tobacco, corn, and other staple crops once grew.

Appalachian wine country is a space of conversation between new and old ideas about community, farming, rusticity, class, and sustainability. There are places where the story of wine is woven into the story of Appalachian communities and connects mountain landscapes to emergent practices of hope, skill, craft, science, and innovation—often reflecting the craft beverage scene that rhetorician Jeff Rice sees as a cultural holdover from when the "Arts & Crafts fostered the ever-present critique of consumption by situating the industrial as always antithetical to the artisanal. The industrial is impure; the artisanal is pure. Thus is one craft rhetoric still circulated in craft discourse related to food and beverage cultures."[10] In many cases, the idea is to use both the past and the present to enable the future, such as a handful of farmhouse wineries making organic wines with renewable energy. For example, McRitchie Winery and Ciderworks, located in the Yadkin Valley AVA of North Carolina, prides itself on its sustainable and low-impact practices. Between the vines, orchards, kitchen garden, and energy-efficient tasting room, this vineyard and cidery pays as much scrupulous attention to its footprint on the land as it does to the quality of its products. Using gravity-flow techniques in its barrel/bottling room and landscaping designed as a bee and butterfly habitat, this business promotes stewardship of the planet, the region, and the wine industry itself—making way for modern Appalachian identity politics based in industry practices.

Each winery has its own identity, including the tasting room experience and winemaking and vineyard management styles; however, in every winery studied, we found Appalachian cultural rhetorics were of concern from the moment we drove onto the property or entered the tasting room. For some wineries, the cultural rhetorics center around environmental and cultural sustainability. For others, the cultural rhetorics reproduce an Old World narrative or class-based nostalgia. Still for others, the focus is on the region's farming history and rustic heritage. These cultural moves play out in label art, architecture, aesthetics, winemaking styles, and use/refuse of local music, food, and art. In sum, in addition to being bastions of delicious wines, Appalachia's wine trails are rich rhetorical landscapes laden with cultural signifiers aimed at framing the grape as rooted to the region's past as well as its future. And to that, we can raise a glass.

NOTES

1. Greg Dickinson, "Joe's Rhetoric: Finding Authenticity at Starbucks," *Rhetoric Society Quarterly* 32, no. 4 (Autumn 2002): 7.

2. Ashli Quesinberry Stokes and Wendy Atkins-Sayre, *Consuming Identity: The Role of Food in Redefining the South* (Jackson: University Press of Mississippi, 2016), 91. See also Thornstein Veblen, *The Theory of the Leisure Class*, rev. ed. (Dover Publications, 1994).

3. Phil Bratta and Malea Powell, "Introduction to the Special Issue: Entering the Cultural Rhetorics Conversations," *Enculturation* 21 (April 20, 2016), www.enculturation.net/entering-the-cultural-rhetorics-conversations.

4. "About Us," http://nativevineswinery.com. North Carolina Department of Agriculture and Consumer Services, "North Carolina Wine History," http://www.ncagr.gov/markets/ncwine/about-us/nc-wine-history.html.

5. North Carolina Department of Agriculture and Consumer Services, "About Us," http://www.ncagr.gov/markets/ncwine/about-us.html. Virginia Wine Marketing Office, "Virginia Wine," https://www.virginiawine.org.

6. Dickinson, "Joe's Rhetoric," 10.

7. Stokes and Atkins-Sayre, *Consuming Identity*, 101.

8. Alex Franklin, Julie Newton, and Jesse C. McEntee, "Moving beyond the Alternative: Sustainable Communities, Rural Resilience and the Mainstreaming of Local Food," *Local Environment* 16, no. 8 (September 2011): 776.

9. Colman Andrews, "101 Best Wineries in America 2017," *The Daily Meal*, August 2017, https://www.thedailymeal.com/drink/101-best-wineries-america-2017.

10. Jeff Rice, "Craft Rhetoric," *Communication and Critical/Cultural Studies* 12, no. 2 (June 2015): 219.

Chapter 14

"The Reason We Make These Deep-Fat-Fried Treats": In Conversation with the Rosettes of Helvetia, West Virginia

Emily Hilliard

IT'S A chilly Friday morning in February and I'm standing over a cast-iron pot of hot oil in Eleanor Betler's farmhouse kitchen, just outside Helvetia, West Virginia. Simon and Garfunkel's familiar refrain, "They've all—come—to look for A-merrr-ica!" rings out over the oil sizzles, and the bright kitchen smells of grease and sugar. I hold a long-stemmed tool that resembles a branding iron with an eight-petaled floral design on the end. It looks like a miniature stained-glass window without the glass. Eleanor takes my picture with my camera, her terrier Jazzy bouncing around at my feet.

Sharon Rollins and Linda "Bunch" Smith peer over my shoulder
as I dip the iron first into the hot oil, then into a bowl of batter,
and again into the grease. A few seconds later, the batter releases
from the iron as a fully formed rosette, delicate and crispy, with
a rounded top and a hollow shell on the bottom. "There you go!"
Sharon exclaims. "Keep the iron hot, dip the grease off of it, and
don't cover it up," says Eleanor, "those are the three main rules of
this game!"

Eleanor Betler, at seventy-six, is energetic and spritely, with
short-cropped white hair and eyes that crinkle when she smiles.
She was raised in Cleveland, Ohio, but her mother's family settled
in Helvetia in 1872, and Eleanor spent the summers of her childhood there at her grandparents' home. "I never wanted to go back
to the city. Although [Cleveland] was lovely at the time and a nice
place to be, I was a Helvetia girl, all my life." Helvetia, population
fifty-nine, is a Swiss community nestled in a high mountain valley
of Randolph County, West Virginia. To call the presence of a Swiss
community in a remote area of the Mountain State unlikely would
be a denial of the history and impact of the waves of immigration
and relocation to Central Appalachia by diverse cultural groups.
In fact, there were several Swiss settlements scattered across the
region in the late nineteenth century.[1] But what makes Helvetia
unusual resides not only in the physical preservation of the colorful 1869 alpine village but also in something less tangible. There is
a creative enchantment about the place, exuding from the artful
touches on the hand-painted signs peppered through the village,
the camaraderie of the Helvetia Star Band (now in its fifth generation), and the friendly competition on display in the canned good,
embroidery, and prize tomato entries at the annual agricultural
fair. The intimacy of this community whose families have been
neighbors, friends, and colleagues for generations is its own form
of magic.

When Eleanor married her husband, Bud, in 1961, she got her
"dream come true" and they moved to the old Helvetia hilltop farm
where she's lived ever since. Though Bud passed away in 2010,

Eleanor remains in the comfortable farmhouse where they raised their children. A black-and-white photo of a young Eleanor cutting cinnamon bread hangs next to a tile trivet that reads "Eleanor's Kitchen," marking it as her domain. She serves as the community's historian, managing the Helvetia History Project and Archives housed in a log cabin schoolhouse adjacent to the public library on the historic square. Eleanor, Sharon, and Bunch are all members of the Helvetia Farm Women's Club, which leads community service projects and hosts fund-raisers like the annual ramp supper. Today they are gathered in Eleanor's kitchen to make rosettes and *hozablatz*, or "knee patches," a thin and crispy rectangular fried dough, to serve to locals and guests at tomorrow's square dance. I'm here to document that process for the West Virginia Folklife Program and the Southern Foodways Alliance Oral History Program. Though I've been visiting Helvetia since 2011, interviewed Eleanor over the phone last year, and recognize Sharon from her volunteer work at Helvetia's Hütte Swiss Restaurant, this is the first time meeting the three of them in person.

This Saturday's square dance is not just one of the regular monthly dances held in the Helvetia Community Hall, but part of the community's pre-Lenten holiday, *Fasnacht* (translating as "Fast night")—an amalgam of the traditional Swiss Fasnacht and *Sechelauten*, a rite of spring. Helvetia's take on the event is, like most things in Helvetia, a homespun affair, where locals and visitors don homemade papier-mâché masks and process in a lampion parade between the two town dance halls (participants carry small paper lanterns a distance of about two blocks). They also compete for miniature handmade felt Swiss flags in a mask contest, enjoy homemade fried pastries, square-dance under an effigy of Old Man Winter, and at the stroke of midnight, cut the old man from the rafters and burn him on the bonfire outside to a triumphant a capella rendition of John Denver's "Country Roads."

"The reason we make these deep-fat-fried treats is because it's Fat Tuesday, before the Lenten fast," Eleanor tells me. "They would eat rich foods for the last time for forty days. People don't do that so much anymore in general, but here [in Helvetia] it was a general thing. They didn't dance during Lent and they had a big celebration before Ash Wednesday. And then it was shut off until Easter Sunday." Today, Fasnacht doesn't feel so much like a last hurrah before a period of austerity as it does a bright spot in the dead of winter, intended both to reinforce cultural identity for locals and to lure wintertime tourists to the secluded town. Nevertheless, the tradition of eating fried rosettes, hozablatz, and yeast-raised donuts has remained part of the Fasnacht celebration. The treats are served on a side table during the dance as attendees jockey to get to them; they disappear quickly.

Sitting open on Eleanor's table is a well-worn copy of *Oppis Guet's Vo Helvetia* (translating as *Something Good from Helvetia*), a cookbook of community recipes collected by town matriarch and Hütte cofounder Eleanor Mailloux (1917–2011) for the Helvetia Centennial in 1969, the year after Fasnacht was revived as a public holiday.[2] The book is a dog-eared standby in all Helvetia home kitchens. The recipe for rosettes is listed just under a recipe for "Old Fashioned Fruit Cake," both originating from the kitchen of Alma Burky. "The Rosette iron we use came from Switzerland with the Burkies a century ago. It is well aged!!!" reads the typed headnote. Underneath the recipe, Eleanor has written an addendum in her looped cursive, "My Grandma, Anne McNeal told me her secret to crispiness is adding about a Tablespoon of bourbon." To the ingredient list of cream, eggs, and flour, she's added "1 T. whisky." While the necessary ingredients are minimal, the process requires some practice, not to mention the special rosette iron. As is often the case with community cookbooks whose intended audience is the home cooks of the community itself, the instructions are sparse:

> Beat cream, eggs and flour together until light. Heat fat very hot for deep frying. Rosette iron should be in the fat heating at the same time. Dip hot Rosette iron into batter, almost to the top edge of iron. Put immediately into hot fat and remove iron as soon as Rosette slips off. Brown on

both sides (this is easier than it sounds—and is great fun)[.]
Put on paper and sprinkle with sugar.

There's no specification of type of fat or sugar, nor timing or temperature (Eleanor keeps her oil at 385 degrees Fahrenheit and has
a staple indicating that temperature on her thermometer so she
remembers). Though to an outsider the recipe's terseness could
feel like a frustrating omission, this assumption of knowledge,
communicated through the text, is a way of ensuring that rosettes
are not parsed from their local story and oral history. In Helvetia,
rosette-making is a process best learned in person rather than from
a book. Eleanor remembers her aunt and mother making rosettes
for Easter and when she visited in the summer, but when Eleanor
moved to Helvetia after she got married, she relearned how to
make them from her family members. "Fasnacht needed them, so
I went down to my grandmother and her older daughter to renew
my knowledge. And I just like doing it. . . . I need to teach Jerryanne
so she can do [it] for the next generation."

The lack of specificity in the recipe inspires conversation,
even for those in the know. As Bunch stacks the cooled rosettes
and prepares to dust them with sugar, she asks Eleanor what type
to use. "Some of the people use regular and some use powdered
sugar," Eleanor replies. I chime in, "I remember last year when I
interviewed you, you said, 'Well, you use what you've got!'" "That's
right!" Eleanor says, and the women agree, completing each other's
sentences. "Up here you use what you've got, cause . . ." "Or what
your neighbor has!" "You have to improvise once in a while." "You
can't get to the grocery store very often." They decide to sprinkle
powdered sugar on the rosettes, with the caveat that if they don't
like them this time, they'll try something different next year.
They're casual about the process, negotiating the various steps
anew each time they gather to make them. But Eleanor, who grew
up with the fried confections and learned the process from her
family matriarchs, is deferred to as the authority. When the Betlers
were raising and butchering hogs on the farm, Eleanor fried her

rosettes in lard—they had plenty on hand. But now that she doesn't keep pigs, lard is expensive to purchase, and she only buys it to make soap. She made the switch to frying rosettes in vegetable oil not just for economy but also for health reasons. "Not that deep-fat-fried is healthy. Whatsoever," she wryly adds. In the evolution of her rosette-making process, Eleanor enacts folklorist Henry Glassie's definition of tradition as "the creation of the future out of the past."[3] While ingredients, techniques, styles, and tools change according to time and context, the tradition persists, with Eleanor as its creative agent.

With a pint of medium cream, six eggs, two cups of flour, and if you're smart, a tablespoon of whiskey, the rosette recipe yields a deceivingly large quantity of rosettes. When I asked the women how much it makes, Sharon responded, "A bucketful! It's the way we measure here." "That's the Swiss way of measuring," Eleanor jested. Indeed, she, Sharon, and Bunch stacked them in a large bucket—the high sides protect the delicate fritters and make it easy to transport them. The recipe yield indicates that in Helvetia, rosettes are intended for a large gathering—a special occasion that will feed many. Aside from Fasnacht, Eleanor sometimes makes them for Easter, but only when she has company. "It's too much for just me," she says. She's also made double batches for Helvetian weddings. Rosettes are a social food—a treat you never eat alone—and as the recipe denotes, their creation is part of the communal fun.

Helvetians have an extremely local identity. They're Helvetians first, West Virginians and Appalachians second. Eleanor Betler told me, "We are not a typical Appalachian culture, but we are part of its history and a living history at that." In Helvetia, food is a carrier of that localized identity. The Hütte Swiss Restaurant is a community institution and the public face of the town. Open daily since the late 1960s, it offers a range of Swiss dishes from *rosti* to *sauerbraten* to homemade sauerkraut on its menu. In its fifty years of operation, the Hütte has played a crucial role in the preservation and continuation of the community's foodways traditions, shared narrative, and cohesion. Eighteen-year-old Morgan Rice, who waitresses at the restaurant and whose father is a co-owner, told me, "With the Hütte, it wouldn't be the same if people came to Helvetia or if I come home from college and I don't smell the sausage cooking or I don't smell the chicken cooking because that just gives it the Swiss feel." Locals treat the restaurant like their communal dining room, stopping by the kitchen to serve themselves a cup of coffee in the morning, placing their orders from memory (no need for the menu), and gathering around one of the Hütte's woodstoves for a glass of homemade wine and an impromptu music session when there's a power outage. While Fasnacht has evolved from the private holiday that it once was to the small tourist destination it is today, the fried treats made by the women of the community are a subtle yet powerful symbol of tradition and ritual. They provide an edible link to Helvetian heritage, whether the consumer is from Helvetia or away. When you take a bite of a delicate, handmade rosette, you partake in the place and, consciously or not, experience a sensory understanding of its domestic history. Eleanor put it more practically: "Food is a very important part of any Helvetia event, because when you come at least an hour from any large town, you want food! It's what really brings people here."

I'm not from West Virginia or Appalachia, let alone Helvetia. I grew up in northern Indiana, in a rust belt town surrounded by Amish country cornfields. Before moving to West Virginia from Washington, D.C., I had spent time in West Virginia for work and play but had never lived here. Well aware of the history of cultural, economic, and resource extraction in the region, when I took the position of state folklorist, my title felt uncomfortable, presumptuous. Though I intended to make West Virginia my home, my outsider status weighed heavy; I didn't want my work to be considered exploitive. But when I began doing interviews, sat down in someone's living room, enjoyed a bowl of soup at their kitchen table, or handed my camera over and let them document me, my anxiety faded. It requires trust to welcome a stranger into your home, especially a stranger with a recorder and camera, and

I try to reciprocate that trust in my fieldwork. This is grounded in the collaborative ethnographic methods I was taught, which value both consultant and folklorist as equals.[4] Each party is an expert in their own experience. I still continually assess my perspective and check my assumptions, but in moments of difference—between insiders and outsiders, or across cultures, class, or race—I rely upon that methodology, which minimizes labels and values individual relationships over structures of separation.

In this work that regularly takes me into communities not my own, I'm accustomed to being humbled, finding ease in unfamiliarity. I ask questions—whether deliberately or inadvertently—that must sometimes seem so obvious to insiders. But my basic inquiries can be the key that unlocks an interview, an opportunity for us to reach a common understanding and deeply consider a seemingly simple element of a cultural practice or identity, something an insider might take for granted or has never fully explained before. New understandings arise out of our conversations, just as they do in the making of a recipe. In both, there's a list of steps to follow, but the improvisation required in a conversation or a cooking process is actually what makes the final product. Both are creative remakings of the world. Sometimes, as with Bunch, Sharon, and Eleanor, that remaking happens between individuals within the same community, but there's also a value in dialogues between those of different backgrounds. In the negotiation of understanding, revelations emerge that allow us to conceptualize or understand our own identity, culture, or work in a new way. Like the process of making rosettes, interviews and fieldwork are casual conversations, discussed and negotiated at each step. There's a prescribed structure, but the interpretation is a product of the specific individuals involved, unique every time.

When I first wrote about rosettes for NPR, some readers commented that rosettes are not in fact Swiss, but Scandinavian. Eleanor said, "The rosettes, I don't even know if that's a Swiss thing. Well, it has to be because everybody, every family has a big rosette iron that they brought from Switzerland, so it must have been very important." I figured that they could have both Swiss and Scandinavian roots, considering the history of western European and Scandinavian migration and travel. When I looked up "rosettes" in the *Oxford Companion to Sugar and Sweets*, though, I found out that those migratory patterns and origin stories of rosettes may be wider than I imagined. Adam Balic writes, "The fritters are known as *rosetbakkelser* (rosettes) in Norway, *struvor* in Sweden, and *dok jok* in Thailand [which have black and white sesame seeds in the batter, along with tapioca and rice flour]. Turkey has *demir tatlisi* (iron pudding), Tunisia *chebbak el-janna* (windows of paradise), and Kerala *achappam*. Afghani fritters are called *kulcha-e-panjerei* (window biscuits); in Indonesia they are known as *kembang goyang* (swaying flowers)."[5] Other analogs include Columbian *solteritas con crema*, and Iranian *nan-e panjerehi*, which are made with cardamom and rosewater. Sri Lankan *kokis* or *koekjes* call for rice flour, coconut milk, and turmeric and are fried in coconut oil. When I asked Eleanor if she knew of these rosette equivalents in other cultures, she said she wasn't surprised—growing up Cleveland in a Slavic neighborhood, she often found similarities between her own family's Irish and Swiss heritage, the traditions of her Slavic neighbors, and those of other immigrant communities in the city. Mirroring the symbol of the rosette pattern with eight lines radiating out from a single center, connected by a common circle, rosettes connect Helvetia to cultural communities across the globe.

In an essay entitled "Moulds for Shaping and Decorating Food in Turkey," food historian Priscilla Mary Isin notes that fritters shaped with long-stemmed patterned irons date back at least five centuries; they are first mentioned in print in 1570 by the Italian Renaissance chef Bartolomeo Scappi. Many varieties of fried pastries, whether made with an iron or not, can be traced to the Middle Ages, when open fire cooking was more common and accessible than oven baking. I imagine this may be why they were popular in the log cabin kitchens of early Helvetia too. A singular point of origin for rosettes and their kin has not been pinpointed, but Isin posits that they may have originated in the Islamic world, possibly rural Turkey, and spread from there. In some cases, fritters came to areas through colonization, as was the case with Sri Lankan *koekjes,* which Dutch colonists brought to the country in the mid-seventeenth to late-eighteenth centuries. The resemblance between cattle branding irons and rosette irons may not in fact be coincidental; in the city of Van and its surrounding areas in western Turkey, each family had a distinctive fritter iron pattern, comparable to livestock branding symbols indicating particular familial ownership. These custom irons were fashioned by local blacksmiths to the specifications of each family. Adam Balic notes that in Europe the irons were sometimes made in the form of coats of arms, and in England they were called "stock fritters" or "fritters of arms."[6]

While Eleanor Betler doesn't recall any familial proprietary rosette irons in Helvetia, coat of arms symbols are a signature element in Helvetia's visual culture. The exterior of the Community Hall that houses the monthly square dances, as well as Fasnacht, the Ramp Supper, the Community Fair, and other local events, is adorned with wooden hand-painted coats of arms that symbolize the Swiss cantons of each original family. Helvetia also has a signature crest, created by Eleanor Mailloux. The Swiss cross appears in the upper left corner on a red background, with a heart and flower on the opposite side, painted in green and yellow. Mailloux's granddaughter Clara Lehmann co-owns the Helvetia- and Chicago-based film production company, Coat of Arms Post, the moniker alluding to the symbol's significance in Lehmann's hometown. The company sells its coat of arms–themed card decks at the Kultur Haus. When I visited Helvetia for the Maple Syrup Festival in nearby Pickens this spring, I stopped by the Helvetia Archives and Museum table, where Eleanor Betler was sitting with fellow historians Anna May Chandler and Cheryl Mail. I told them about the Turkish fritter irons and their distinctive familial patterns. "It's like our porch railings!" Anna excitedly replied, explaining that when the first families built their homes in Helvetia, each had a particular porch railing gingerbread pattern that indicated whose home it was.

She pulled up over a dozen photos on the archive computer, each depicting a family's unique railing design.[7] The Burkys' railings feature a heart cut out of the center of each rail, the Koerners' are designed in a wide hourglass, and what's thought to be the Kerlen/ Kuenzler families' are shaped like an angel's harp, mirrored on the top and bottom. Even relative newcomers, like Dave Whipp, who moved to Helvetia after retirement, have adopted the tradition—his balcony railings form two faces in profile, creating a wine glass between them (Dave is an avid home winemaker).

In the early immigrant community of Helvetia, material culture was important—a value that persists today as evinced by the fine embroidery, furs, and other crafts exhibited at the annual Community Fair, the wool yarn and blankets produced by the Helvetia Shepherd's Association, and the Fasnacht masks, displayed and preserved in the Kultur Haus. Living in a rural place where a trip to the store is an hour drive or more, objects are all the more valuable. The original families could only bring their most important possessions with them from Switzerland, so it's notable that rosette irons were among them. Today, rosette irons are found on display at the Hütte restaurant and in the homes of the McNeals (Eleanor's grandmother's family), the Burkys, the Detweilers, and the Betlers, among others. Most irons have an eight-petaled pattern, though others are shaped like stars and scalloped circles and squares. Eleanor's favorite iron came from Amish country in Ohio—it has a nonstick coating and is somewhat smaller than the one her mother got her from Pier 1 in Cleveland or her family's steel heirloom iron, so is better suited for making a large quantity for the Fasnacht crowd.

I also told Clara Lehmann that Turkish rosette irons are patterned as family crests. Though she, like Eleanor, doesn't believe this was ever the case in Helvetia, she liked the idea, and asked a local blacksmith if he would make customized rosette irons—including a commemorative iron—to sell at that year's Helvetia Community Fair. While folklorist Henry Glassie asserts that tradition is the "creation of the future out of the past," I'd phrase it another way—that tradition puts the past and the future in conversation. Traditions mutate and evolve as they encounter and enter into dialogue with influences inside and out, global and local: the grandmother who adds whiskey to the printed recipe; the friends who decide to try powdered sugar instead of granulated this year; the home cook who swaps her lard for vegetable oil and an heirloom tool for a smaller, more practical version; the midwesterner folklorist who learns to make rosettes from the home cook, finds her own iron on Etsy, and introduces them to her friends; the granddaughter who learns about a Turkish tradition from said midwesterner folklorist and adapts it for her West Virginia Swiss community. And what better symbol for this than a rosette iron—a physical embodiment of that past and future negotiation? Metal forged centuries ago will make fresh rosettes tomorrow.

NOTES

1. David H. Sutton, *Helvetia: The History of a Swiss Village in the Mountains of West Virginia* (Morgantown: West Virginia University Press, 2010).

2. Eleanor Mailloux, ed., *Oppis Guet's Vo Helvetia* (Helvetia: Alpenrose Garden Club, 1969).

3. Henry Glassie, "Tradition," in Eight Words for the Study of Expressive Culture, ed. Burt Feintuch (Urbana: University of Illinois Press, 2003), 177.

4. I was trained to use the term "consultant" for ethnographic interviewees/participants/informants, as per Luke Eric Lassiter's *Chicago Guide to Collaborative Ethnography.* This term implies an equal dynamic between folklorist/ethnographer and consultant, as both are experts in their own field and experience. For more on reciprocal or collaborative ethnography, see Luke Eric Lassiter, *Chicago Guide to Collaborative Ethnography* (Chicago: University of Chicago Press, 2005). See also Elaine Lawless, *Holy Women, Wholly Women: Sharing Ministries through Life Stories and Reciprocal Ethnography* (Philadelphia: University of Philadelphia Press, 1993).

5. Emily Hilliard, "Fat Tuesday: The Many Different Doughnuts of Mardi Gras," *NPR Kitchen Window: A Weekly Peek into the Kitchen with Tasty Tales and Recipes,* February 26, 2014, http://www.npr.org

/2014/02/26/282908382/fat-tuesday-the-many-different-doughnuts
-of-mardi-gras. Adam Balic, "Fritters," in *The Oxford Companion to
Sugar and Sweets*, ed. Darra Goldstein (New York: Oxford University
Press, 2015), 276–77.

6. Priscilla Mary Işın, "Moulds for Shaping and Decorating Food in
Turkey," in *Food and Material Culture: Proceedings of the Oxford Sympo-
sium on Food and Cookery 2013*, ed. Mark McWilliams (Devon: Prospect
Books, 2014), 184. Mary Işın, *Sherbet and Spice: The Complete Story of
Turkish Sweets and Desserts* (New York: I.B. Tauris, 2013), 10–11. Balic,
"Fritters," 276–77.

7. See Porch Railings document held in the Helvetia Genealogy
Archives, http://helvetiawv.com/Genealogy/Index.html.

Poems

How to Kill a Rooster

Rebecca Gayle Howell

Because he's spurred you
grab him by his neck and his legs

Hold him in both your hands
Look him in the eye

Let him ask
if you are to kill him today

then tell him yes   say *yes*
with your own eye

How to Kill a Rooster

just before you take him
to the clothes line

and tie him up
by his yellow feet

Take a blade
Cut his throat

Watch his blood drip
to the ground

Watch his wings spread
and flap and flap and

while you watch this desperate bird
and think to yourself

I will never be like him

remember in the end you will
drop him in boiling water

pluck each of his oily feathers
between your fingers

Remember in the end
you will taste him

for good

How to Kill a Hen

Rebecca Gayle Howell

Enter the night coop
whistling

Through your teeth
sing

In this awful world of sorrow
sing

In this wicked path of sin

Tuck her
under your arm

and walk away
from the laying birds

the cuckold-morning
rising in their dumb wings

Walk away from sleep

Make sure her hollow bones
alone will be warmed by it

your wordless bellows
breast

How to Kill a Hen

For this is your gift to her

Tell her
you never think of tomorrow

Tell her
what you'd lose in the end

Enter the night coop
whistling

Leave whistling
Climb the dust hill

When you get up
to the house

ring once the orbit
of your failing

Over your head
a breaking neck

For this is your gift to her:

You can hear your savior calling
barefaced and feather red

Afterword

Ronni Lundy

Miso.

It was not an ingredient in my mother's kitchen, and certainly not in that of either of my Appalachian grandmothers. Yet it is a significant addition to one of the most intriguing recipes in *Victuals: An Appalachian Journey, with Recipes,* a cookbook whose mission was to present a genuine taste of the Mountain South, one rooted in traditions yet dynamic in reality.

The miso isn't there just for novelty, or even to underscore the fact that contemporary mountain cooks have access to more ingredients than their forebears did. It's there, first of all, because chef Ian Boden's addition of crumbles of a rich, sour, salty banana bread to an otherwise classic banana pudding gives it a distinct twist of flavor, a twist I like to call "Appalachian Umami."

Afterword

Umami is the Japanese term for the meaty essence that is now recognized as a "fifth flavor," along with salty, sweet, sour, and bitter.[1] It's what gives succulent body and soul to a plain pot of dried beans simmered low and slow with just an inch or two of white bacon in it. Throw a handful of chopped white or green onion on the top of such soup beans, or add a spoonful of chow chow, and the result is a dish that my mother would have approvingly said "has got a *whang* to it."

That meaty *whang* is what I call Appalachian Umami, the term I proposed to a group of fellow diners one night at Ian's restaurant, The Shack, in Staunton, Virginia. We included chefs Travis Milton and Anna Bogle, foodwriter Kendra Bailey Morris, regional scholars and activists Lora Smith and Amelia Kirby—all born and raised in the southern Appalachians. And we greedily agreed that Ian's pudding had the taste of those mountains in spades. We further noted that while soybeans were not in the pantheon of beloved traditional mountain beans, the process by which they are turned into miso—fermentation—is, in fact, the source of the distinct umami-with-whang-to-it of some of the unique foods of the region: pickled corn and sour beans, kraut and cider, sock sausage and the homemade fermentations from a variety of fruits that give mountain vinegar pies a range of flavors. Ours was a discussion and discovery almost as satisfying as that pudding.

And like most great conversations shared around a mountain table, the story hardly ended there. Some months later I sat in my kitchen with a young photographer from Asheville, Mike Belleme. As we shared the cornbread and cobbler I'd baked for his photos for a *New York Times* piece on cast-iron cooking, we also swapped stories. Turns out Mike is the son of counterculture parents who moved to Western North Carolina in the late 1970s. They're part of the larger hippie migration prefigured in Gurney Norman's classic Appalachian picaresque, *Divine Right's Trip*, published initially in 1971 in the margins of *The Whole Earth Catalog*, and in paperback from Bantam in 1972.[2] Norman's hero, D.R. Davenport, wanders and is lost until he connects himself to Appalachian soil (by reclaiming it from strip-mined surfaces with earthworms and rabbit manure).

Norman's vision was fiction that became grounded in fact as southern Appalachia offered fertile ground for 1970s back-to-the-landers, many of whom, like Mike's parents, found ways to make a life here through the making and marketing of food. But John and Jan Belleme's story had a particular tang for me when Mike shared it, as they'd chosen to establish, in the foothills of the Blue Ridge range, the American Miso Company.

The choice wasn't arbitrary. As foodwriter Keia Mastrianni explained in a 2016 article in *Edible Asheville,* John and Jan studied hands-on for eight months with a fourth-generation miso-making family in the mountain foothills of Japan's Tochigi prefecture. On their return, they found a 120-acre farm in Rutherfordton, North Carolina, a region that mimicked the climate and growing conditions they knew from Japan, and proved to be the perfect place for producing high-quality, organic miso. The company has been doing so now for more than three-and-a-half decades, selling close to 700,000 pounds annually, making it the world's largest manufacturer of organic miso.[3]

This is not the first Asian/Appalachian foodways connection, as anyone who has studied the harvesting, marketing, and uses of mountain ginseng over the past century can attest. Nor is it likely to be the last as Appalachian growers currently explore the profitable viability of growing and marketing wasabi (and as a new generation of young mountain eaters acknowledge its value as a *whang* with a kick to it).

Are miso and wasabi traditional Appalachian ingredients? Of course not. At least, not yet, because we do have to ask, Just when does tradition begin? Sweet sorghum syrup, the very definition of so many iconic mountain foods, from apple stack cake, to gingerbread, to biscuits dolloped with it swirled in fresh cream butter, didn't come to the mountains until the Civil War. At what point did it stop being a novelty and become a mountain basic? What about those Red Hots your granny started putting in her apple butter?

What about pickled baloney? Pepperoni rolls? Goulash? Chili buns and West Virginia Slaw Dogs?

What about the enticing, golden, savory bacon grease you've heated to sizzling in your great-grandmother's cast-iron skillet, and poured into your cornbread batter? Bacon grease was once an immigrant's ingredient, you know; not one that the original native dwellers in Appalachia used to make their pones. And that skillet was at one time a fotched-on, newfangled implement, as novel to the region as a slow cooker in the early 1970s.

Like the miso in the banana pudding, many of these new ingredients, new tools and techniques, new stories, fit into the already existing landscapes, foodscapes, and narratives of Appalachia. And over time, they become a piece of the narrative of the region. They both challenge and deepen our understanding of what it means to be from and of the southern mountains. And they underscore that the people here live, as they always have, in a place where tradition always dances with diversity, yielding to change.

From the earliest days of its "discovery" by explorers from Europe to the present when its exploiters continue to name it and claim it, Appalachia and its people have been told what their story is supposed to be. Misnamed by the Spanish in the 1500s (after a northern Florida native tribe), given a specious "elegy" in 2016, mocked in cartoons, demonized in film and photography, these stories "about" us continue to bewilder and trouble those of us who come from a history and reality that is quite different.

We challenge such stories, then, by telling our own, our truth. We bring our particulars to the table, like a family that stretches over generations, coming to the reunion. Some of us bring chicken that has been home skillet-fried, some of us bring a bucket or a box. We discover both the difference and the kinship in chow chow and kimchee. We marvel at the ingenuity of our vegan cousins who "bacon-up" their beans with tamari or smoked Spanish paprika. And by sharing foods and traditions that were handed down, we honor the memories of ancestors: those who were native; those who came from Africa and Ireland; the English who were gentry and those who came indentured; the Germans who brought their crocks for fermenting; the Swiss, Italian, Hungarian, Asturian, and Welsh miners, masons, and millworkers; the Quakers and the Huguenots seeking religious freedom; the brides of soldiers from Korea and Vietnam; the workers from Mexico; heck, even the recent Brooklynites.

Everything we have been handed down, from cookbook to rosette wand, everything we receive, from egg roll to taco, everything we jones for, from red hot hotdogs to candies, becomes a piece of our history, a thread in the story leading to more story.

Sitting at the Appalachian table we can taste the proof of a strong, lasting, surprisingly diverse, and infinitely textured history. Passing our foods and our stories to one another, and extending them to you, we can see our way into the future.

NOTES

1. Hannah Goldfield, "You Think You Know Umami," *New Yorker*, March 19, 2015, https://www.newyorker.com/culture/culture-desk/you-think-you-know-umami.

2. John Deck, "Divine Right's Trip," *New York Times*, July 2, 1972, https://www.nytimes.com/1972/07/02/archives/divine-rights-trip-by-gurney-norman-302-pp-new-york-the-dial-press.html.

3. Keia Mastrianni, "The Miso Masters," *Edible Asheville*, http://www.edibleasheville.com/miso-masters/.

Contributors

COURTNEY BALESTIER is a writer whose work focuses on the intersection of place and identity, particularly in her native Appalachia. Her work has appeared in the *New York Times,* the *New Yorker* online, *Lucky Peach,* and the *Oxford American,* among other publications, and has been nominated for a James Beard Foundation Journalism Award and a Pushcart Prize.

JESSIE BLACKBURN is Associate Professor of English and Director of the Composition and Rhetoric Program at Appalachian State University. She is the author of the forthcoming *Appalachian Terroir: A Rhetorical Approach to New Landscapes* as well as articles in her specialties of cultural, digital, feminist, and Appalachian critical regional rhetorics.

KARIDA L. BROWN is Assistant Professor in the Departments of Sociology and African American Studies at UCLA. She is a sociologist whose research is centered on processes of racialization, subject formation, and the social construction of the self. Her book, *Gone Home: Race and Roots through Appalachia* (UNC Press), examines the intergenerational migration of a cohort of African Americans who migrated throughout Appalachia during the twentieth-century African American Great Migration.

DANILLE ELISE CHRISTENSEN is an Assistant Professor in the Department of Religion & Culture at Virginia Tech. A folklorist, she studies how people position vernacular knowledge, skills, and creativity—especially those forms that have been framed as "domestic"—within hierarchies of value. Her forthcoming book, *Freedom from Want: Home Canning in the American Imagination* (UNC Press), explores who has promoted home canning over the last century and why.

ANNETTE SAUNOOKE CLAPSADDLE, an enrolled member of the Eastern Band of Cherokee Indians, resides in Qualla, North Carolina. National Board Certified, Annette teaches English and Cherokee Studies at Swain County High School, and her debut novel is due out from the University Press of Kentucky in the summer of 2020. She was the recipient of the Morning Star Award for Creative Writing and a finalist for the PEN/Bellwether Prize for Socially Engaged Fiction.

MICHAEL CROLEY was born in the foothills of the Appalachian Mountains and is the author of *Any Other Place: Stories*. The recipient of an NEA Fellowship in Literature in 2016, he teaches creative writing at Denison University.

ELIZABETH S. D. ENGELHARDT is the John Shelton Reed Distinguished Professor of Southern Studies at the University of North Carolina at Chapel Hill. Western North Carolina, where her family has lived since before 1780, has long been central to her research and writing about southern food and gender, most recently in books such as *A Mess of Greens* and *The Larder* and in her work with the Southern Foodways Alliance.

ROBERT GIPE is author of two novels, *Trampoline* and *Weedeater*, and is former director of the Southeast Kentucky Community & Technical College Appalachian Program. He grew up in Kingsport, Tennessee, birthplace of Pal's Sudden Service, and earned his first Pal's sauceburger at age seven, during a time when Pal's gave students a free sauceburger for every A on their report card. All Gipe has achieved since derives in part from this early encouragement.

A native of north-central West Virginia, **SURONDA GONZALEZ** has a passion for uncovering and retelling a good story. That led her to northern Appalachia, where she completed an advanced degree focusing on the history of immigration, social policy, and gender in the United States. She continues to research and write about the region and to pursue stories hidden in plain sight.

EMILY HILLIARD is the West Virginia state folklorist and founding director of the West Virginia Folklife Program at the West Virginia Humanities Council. Her writing and media work have been published by NPR, *Southern Cultures, Ecotone Magazine,* the Southern Foodways Alliance, West Virginia University Press, and others. She is currently at work on a book based on her folklife fieldwork in West Virginia, under contract with Ohio University Press.

REBECCA GAYLE HOWELL's awards include fellowships from United States Artists, the Fine Arts Work Center, and the Carson McCullers Center, as well as a Pushcart Prize. Howell is the poetry editor for *Oxford American;* her most recent book is *American Purgatory.*

Originally from northwest North Carolina, **ABIGAIL HUGGINS** earned an MA in Southern Studies from the University of Mississippi, focusing on foodways, oral history, and Appalachia through her thesis, "Before Me, After Me, Through Me: Stories of Food and Community in Eastern Kentucky." Abigail collaborated with Hindman Settlement School on the East Kentucky Food & Dance Trail as an Appalachian Transition Fellow through the Highlander Research and Education Center and continues to live in eastern Kentucky.

ERICA ABRAMS LOCKLEAR is Professor of English at the University of North Carolina at Asheville. A Western North Carolina native, she writes about food, Appalachia, and the South. Her first book, *Negotiating a Perilous Empowerment: Appalachian Women's Literacies,* explores the identity conflicts that literacy attainment can cause for mountain women. Her current project, *Appalachia on the Table*, investigates representations of mountain food from the late nineteenth century to today.

RONNI LUNDY is the author of the James Beard award-winning *Victuals: An Appalachian Journey, with Recipes*, and the groundbreaking *Shuck Beans, Stack Cakes, and Honest Fried Chicken*, both cookbooks that delve deeply into the foodways of the southern Appalachians. She is a founder of the Southern Foodways Alliance and the Appalachian Food Summit. Born in Corbin, Kentucky, her roots extend through the southern mountains across multiple generations.

A native of Harlan County, former Kentucky Poet Laureate (2015–16) **GEORGE ELLA LYON** writes in many genres for readers of all ages. Recent collections include *She Let Herself Go* (LSU Press, 2012) and *Many-Storied House* (University Press of Kentucky, 2013).

JEFF MANN has published five books of poetry, *Bones Washed with Wine, On the Tongue, Ash, A Romantic Mann*, and *Rebels;* two collections of essays, *Edge* and *Binding the God;* a book of poetry and memoir, *Loving Mountains, Loving Men;* six novels, *Fog, Purgatory, Cub, Salvation, Country*, and *Insatiable;* and three volumes of short fiction, *A History of Barbed Wire, Desire and Devour*, and *Consent*. He teaches creative writing at Virginia Tech.

DANIEL S. MARGOLIES is Professor and Chair of the History Department at Virginia Wesleyan University, where he teaches courses on globalization, Southern music and culture, borderlands, and beekeeping, among other topics. He is the author or editor of four books and numerous book chapters and articles. Margolies's research encompasses a wide interdisciplinary range from globalized food and music cultures to legal spatiality in American foreign relations to cultural sustainability in Texas-Mexican conjunto music.

Contributors

WILLIAM SCHUMANN is the Director of the Center for Appalachian Studies at Appalachian State University. He is interested in community-based research and sustainability in Appalachia and other rural mountain regions. He is the coeditor of and a contributor to *Appalachia Revisited: New Perspectives on Place, Tradition, and Progress* (University Press of Kentucky).

LORA E. SMITH is the Director of the Appalachian Impact Fund, a place-based social impact investment fund focused on a just and equitable economic transition in the coalfields of Appalachian Kentucky. Smith is a founding member of the Appalachian Food Summit and an author who focuses on food and social justice. Her work has been featured in *Gravy*, the *New York Times*, PUNCH, and NPR's *The Salt*. In 2015, Lora accepted the Southern Foodways Alliance's John Egerton Prize for her work with the Appalachian Food Summit and local food movements in Central Appalachia.

EMILY WALLACE is the art director and deputy editor for *Southern Cultures* quarterly at the Center for the Study of the American South. She is also the author and illustrator of *Road Sides: An Illustrated Companion to Dining and Driving in the American South* (University of Texas Press).

CRYSTAL WILKINSON is the award-winning author of *The Birds of Opulence* (winner of the 2016 Ernest J. Gaines Prize for Literary Excellence), *Water Street*, and *Blackberries, Blackberries*. Nominated for both the Orange Prize and the Hurston/Wright Legacy Award, she currently teaches at the University of Kentucky, where she is Associate Professor of English in the MFA in Creative Writing Program.